AF272212

« You have a Good one! »

HEIKE THIEME – Ylva

Training in "Freedom" just Be YOURSELF,
immerse yourself in romance
pay your rent with admiration
the spectator can be a guest.

God who has implanted mercy in us. He has
made us a reason to help those who need us,
our origins and humanity, which is no longer
present in most people.

Modern Life Today!

Imprint

Copyright - This text has been edited with the greatest care. The publication is protected by copyright. All rights reserved by the author. No part of the book may be reproduced in any form by photocopy, film or other process without written permission from the publisher. The rights of reproduction by lecture, radio and television are also reserved.

© 2024 Heike Thieme, production and publishing:
BoD - Books on Demand, Norderstedt ISBN 978-3-7597-7604-4

My father,
the moon,
my mother,
who lives in it.
I became the one that none of them knows.
But that's a good thing !

hi, hello friend! Who knows where you are right now?
I've been very relaxed the last few days, even dreaming of my own mother
living inside me, a beautiful blonde woman. She is always the same figure, a
former neighbor. I felt like she had been adopted from my family all my life,
but she still protects me to this day, warns me about others, explains other
people's thoughts and intentions to me. She also shows me the family
circumstances in which I grew up and how people have developed. This
time she was blonde for once, but the same woman, and protected me again,
warning me that if there was someone who was trying to hurt me, then I had
a duty not to react in the same aggressive way, as long as our connection
remains! I am very proud that many women meet me in dreams and praise
me for every behavior I have shown.

I have a question. I have never been in a relationship with a man or a
woman or anyone else. So I would like to know what someone thinks of
me? Am I perhaps the ego type with a great need for patience, attention and
care? Or am I seen as a transcendental magical sister who silently looks you
in the eye when she has a wish? And who am I after sex? Could the other
person be more interested in getting to know me once these first acts are
over? And what about his or my dislikes, the lower tolerance for actions or
reactions? Am I not a little too interested in all these topics in the whole
world? If I am an open woman, is this man irritated by my jokes, desires and
spontaneity, or is that the reason for leaving me from the start?

I think I know. I am the magically calmer type.

That's it for today,

have a good time, I'm going to prepare myself mentally for a really new good novel, I've wanted to do that for a long time. The lawyer, as usual, is now doing her part of the deal, and maybe I'll get some peace and quiet to paint again.

Anyone who loves his friends,
does not travel to the desert,
does not shit on others,
does not complain as a guest,
does not aspire to the highest offices,
does not cheat public money,
does laugh at all women,
does insist on the power of the church,
does not know what to do,
does not call others by their names,
does hobby horsing,
does it with one of his daughters,
does not show respect for their mischief,
does not make himself into a special being,
does not deserve any special status!

I have a Good One !
I have now gotten to know a whole number of women properly.
This means that the loud ones, the fascist feminists, don't make a big fuss about it because, in their stormy ways and for the sake of nature, they have clearly already met the wrong man. Unfortunately, that only makes them more and more disgruntled. No one had a good time with them. I thought about it quietly for a while. Women who are mostly known in the Rhineland as fascist feminists. Haved a messed up upbringing. But all the facts always come to light. Not all of them manage to get their hands on the sluggish, wealthy yes-man as their prince, who is so oppressed that he spirals into depression and powerlessly escapes from it.

Some experience the exact opposite, and the man teaches them the lesson of a lifetime. No one is given everything in life for free. Some people have a good understanding of human nature and say to themselves that this encounter would definitely have an expiration date even after years, and this woman will come back to the point of fact, as if from then on she had to make her own sandwiches and her sex didn't mean a trophy for the living room shelf because she was too happy to think a clever man was a fool who she didn't train. From then on, the scales fall from her eyes and she realizes that she has chosen the absolutely wrong profession because not all the fascist feminists in the social work field uncritically think everything is admirable and then roll out the red carpet for her for the rest of her life. From this moment of her raging jealousy, she must realize that this is destroying her relationship and that she has blinded herself with her greed for recognition, attention, fame and to make it big on the show!

Women who probably flee their messed-up parents' home and go into wealth. They only seem to have found a saviour, but all material things have fallen silent, and they experience how their escape into what they have and all the beautiful children are just an excuse for not having started to confront themselves first. So anyone who flees the parental home into marriage is always alone at some point. Either because the initially inexperienced man distances himself from her to have an affair, or because the woman becomes aware of her merry-go-round and the little children develop into the same superficial, spoiled, vain, cold-hearted creatures from whom she once fled. She experiences, like a neighbor girl similar to her, who for many years asks for refuge from the bad pig family, for protection, for mental health, acceptance, and a bit of love, and a space for an undamaged childhood, that this mother recognizes in the girl herself, who was on the verge of drowning all her life. And she adopts the child and takes it under her skirt for the rest of her life, vowing to keep it under her skirt, because every child needs emotional protection, so much responsibility she has made her life's work, while her own children were unable to share her luxury, their hearts closed, and the mother soon wished them as far away as possible, until they were gone too, out of sight and out of mind!

Perhaps there is a negative meaning behind the stronghold that a fascist feminist with tits and charm is trying to get hold of, married to a husband on the island of dreams, into comfort, that this woman is always very quickly caught up in unexpected loneliness. This life lie trapped there in the castle, projected as competition against her own daughter, who escapes her mother's coldness alone to the mainland, and on the run blindly falls into the arms of the first psychopath who comes along, who pretends to her how beautiful, how warm, how strong, how familiar it is with him, until the mask falls and the bum can't get anything done and even starts a war of roses over ownership of the child. This means a woman who is demanding, out for love, wants to live a wealthy life, doesn't want to work, is dominant, unkind to backtalk, impatient, got pregnant too early, isn't clear about her emotions, has no control over herself, and complains about having had a bad home, which the poor husband and the children have to make up for all their lives. She sends her whole load of hardship and unresolved childhood onto her husband and child in order to free herself and to pass this negation on to the lives of others. This woman never protects her own children, but only thinks of herself, wants to be celebrated, as the mother animal to be respected forever. The daughter flees, works hard and does not gain any weight. The mother on the island remains, well-fed, a gracious person. A woman who shows psychopathic traits and considers herself irreplaceable.

The do-gooders with the right language
teach elementary school students behavior
swear by non-violent language
meat-free education reverence for the "spice"
facade of politeness, marital sex, Casanova on the side distances
all beautiful animals in the correctness trap !

Tradition displaces religion + language,
culture displaces tradition in my opinion, because some traditions can sometimes be overrated, but culture cannot. I can imagine that celebrities suffer the most, how hard they work to impress the public.

If life were simple,
the band would live next door to us,
our best friend would live above us,
the manager would live in the house next door,
behind a simple wall,
there would be three snack bars on every street,
and there would be a view of the other city
where you only like duck
if you take a weekend trip there.
The cities would all be located by the sea.
And the breast of desire would be
like the salt of the air.

Nobody really knows how to play God
if nobody understands the language of trees
or can interpret the flickering lights behind the lighthouse...!
Obviously I'm an idiot
but maybe there's a chance
that I'm not a huge idiot as I realize
that I learned your language in a real school
and very few people lived my life
are you then a real idiot in my eyes?

My good advice -
Be familiar with your own language before attempting to put yourself in the
shoes of others! I have suffered so much.
Like many people, I am faced with uncertainty before setting off.
I have no goal for the future. Bringing out the inner orientation, as well as
spelling out facts... is the act of instrumentalizing abuse - says the pedophile
in the church!

The language of beating his horse.
Drinking plays on the innermost being.
He always has the last word. The head is buzzing.
The car crashes through the wall. The dog is buried in the lake.
Or suffocated in the trunk.
But the love in their lives never sees the light of day.

You can see that people from Hamburg like to use gutter language, their
dialect is unmistakably colored by macho, beer, St. Pauli, I'll just leave it
there because it's a party weekend to wind down here, then I have to hurry
back, dance with the dolls until I have a heart attack. That's how we know
them.

Equality privileges today dull language in the parents' house
no ideas about childhood also uneducated ways of thinking
but everyone is the same again... bullying
yes, everyone can call themselves the same
even primary school playgrounds are called battlefields
and there are deaths too!
The Frisians always buy their playing cards
ready-mixed in the general store.
Men usually mix so succinctly.
Women with their finer fingers mix upright.
The Japanese mix with one hand and take photos with the other.
Wizards tend to mix as chubby for the show.
The manual dexterity has always been superfluous,
for there is the tongue skill.
If in Germany one understands by partnership
something that only sees the dead Prince Charming,
from whose bowels the woman pulls back her damned wedding ring
in detail, but seen as an operation on the man.
Then I save myself the offer of having to marry a German.

No, if someone asks,
where my ego is located...
I like my belly,
why do I need another one?
I don't go crying into the corner
to hide my pussy.
It's just a tiny little thing
that I put in between
so that I can stay happy inside.
Love for yourself is no longer on the lookout,
so people, don't run away
because you've missed yourself!

A wimp.... is the one who hopes for the right one,
who will take him out of the parental stable,
who he still beats, cracks, and leaves lying there,
A wimp.... who only comes to her mind again,
when 40 years later she is sleeping almost at the gates of the world in a bed
that is just as soft as him, she dreams having a one-off encounter with man,
A wimp.... who is hit on the left foot by her, rolls away, impregnates another
woman, then hopes for a free kick, the old woman is left sitting alone,
and the wimp goes back to his mother,
A wimp.... who can no longer avoid the laughter,
because he is the laughing stock, and will remain so forever !

I QUICKLY GOT THE PICTURE!
I assume that the extermination of Indians at "Wounded Knee"
was comparatively as cruel as the crimes of the Nazis, and I go on to assume
that each side, whether the American West or our European mainland, has
its medal from the death of Sitting Bull the 1973 massacre, only that I was
not willing to travel through the country with a medal trophy, because I
know the people here, "aunt from America" found out about it from me !

It's true our health most important.
We are responsible for ourselves.
The war we live in, is our own war.
The first step to health is quit the war.
The second step is quit the killing thought.
The third step is hinder the negativity in life.
The fourth step is be patient in suffering.
The fifth step is make yourself strong.
The sixth step is healing over years.
The seventh step is not loose contact.
The eighth step is fight for your right.
The ninth step is keep the balance.
The tenth step is live within the system.
The eleventh step is be aware who you are.

At first, a woman cannot talk about her own rape. She can cry. She has nightmares. She has to regain her body. She has to run away. She must never return. After a long period of trust, she has to gain confidence and start to talk. The whole world has to understand what pain this is for women.

It often starts in the parents' home with every form of violence. That is abuse. Then it will be a nasty classmate from school who will jump on you. Then the family fails and declares the victim taboo. Then the woman will trust a stranger, perhaps an American soldier, and get into his car. Then she will follow some people as a confidant to spend an evening together.

It is a battlefield.
Women, don't put up with anything.
The tears are just the beginning !

Flood of the Century !
or Century of Floods ?

It is no longer just...
the flood of the century!
It is the century of floods!

It is no longer just...
the rise of hostile nations.
It is the fomenting of war for WWIII!

It is not just...
the use of a weapon of war!
It is sheer, embarrassing rape!

It is not just...
the avoidance of confrontation with guilt!
It is the stupid rise of schizophrenics!

Was there for a vasectomy,
ONCE and NEVER AGAIN!
Vocational school - no longer a learning system
where only the teacher is at home.
In retrospect, how would I name the vocational school in general?
Place for superfluous provisions for survival with assholes in the:
culture bunker - party bunker - idiot bunker
Protecting the climate or protecting yourself
from it is for those like living a good life,
owning your own home, yacht, bachelor party, accumulating wealth!
Hanging out there and spending your life is better off dying.

- HEIKE THIEME - YLVA -
- Sozialarbeit deutsch/english

Without hope, without sadness. He holds his head down.
Wearily he crouches on the wall. Wearily he sits there and thinks:
Miracles will not happen. Everything stays as it was.
If you don't see anything, you won't be seen.
If you don't see anything, you're invisible.

Steps come, steps go. What kind of people are they?
Why doesn't anyone stop? I am blind and you are blind.
Your heart sends no greetings from the soul to the face.
If I didn't hear your feet, I would think you didn't exist.
Come closer! Sit down, until you sense what blindness is.
Lower your head and lower your eyelids,
until you know what was foreign to you.

And now go! You're in a hurry !
Act as if nothing had happened.
But remember this line:
"If you don't see anything, you won't be seen."
- Erich Kästner -

Two days ago before going to bed...
I met this little fellow, the little weasel,
yesterday under the trees in the avenue
a funny little hedgehog ran past me,
and the rainy summer brings two or three snails to my front door every day,
also twice at midnight a big hare ran towards me in the middle of the road,
braked, and ran back the same way it came,
young deer and small roe deer are also hopping around,
they are not afraid of the city,
ducks present the crowd of children in the middle of intersections,
I am lying there and the eagle is waving to the city from the window,
on the roof there a young heron is clattering its beak,
the wild pigeon lets me talk to it, it loves the topic of children very much,
no one is alone!

I am only now learning to understand that after years of friendship, this seemed strange to me. I thought we always exchanged a little or put into words a little. It seems that we both had the same fear!

We both always feared a close, real bond because we know that a relationship can fall apart even after years if just one wrong sentence is said.

All it takes is a misunderstanding and the whole magic is gone. Even after thirty years, there is no guarantee that a spoken word will turn everything upside down. I think we value each other far too much as friends to end it out of the blue in a human way! We are, will be and probably always have been afraid of not hurting the other person ! Life can be strange. But some things just get too close to you throughout your life. It doesn't matter.
Best wishes, your Heike!

Most time Lovers you meet at the corner, would need a better social worker, not to guess, what would be going on when listen honesyt to the inner heart. You have my absolute agreement ! In life, you never give up and hope. Even the really good ones will experience the sun shining for them again !

I also noticed yesterday that when there are a few clouds, all young people, men, wear the same stupid peaked cap. I mean, we all know about the cell phones in front of their noses, even when they are walking, but that they also wear the same thing?

I remember when, 15 years later, I met a brat outside who was talking about her training as a teacher and I told her that I later published a great book myself about social work and education. She said promptly and banally: "Yes, she would already know, because she knows my book too!" I then said in front of her and someone else who was listening:
"Oh, you actually read it? "Then tell me if you like it?"
The brat replied: "YEEEEEEESSSSS!"

Uhhhah Works ....
"WAHRE UNSCHULD IN DER LIEBE !"
"TRUE INNOCENCE IN LOVE !"

Partner coaching...works like this too,
coach and coachee have not had sex for years,
coachee plays with the man, she sends him to a prostitute,
because she thinks that will save her marriage,
the "making love" was thus
MOVED to another expensive love island
directly to an outsourced pussy..... quite wonderfully
temporarily well rewarded, no less fun,
in the morning they all get up with her,
and in the evening they go again, they stand with her no less,
and then at night he goes back to bed with the coach at home,
and they all go to sleep together.
When people no longer talk to each other.
The feelings of shame outweigh their openness.
"Making love" became embarrassing as they got older.
Then even coach and coachee fall for it,
and the chaos of both idealists begins to falter.

A beauty wilts like a flower, is beauty then power?
Power wilted like a flower.
World of vernissages, therapeutic elite,
of spoiled children and grandchildren, grandchildren's grandchildren,
the car keys belong to the daughter, the power of money thinks
everything and everyone is dear, the born sugar daddy,
the selfies hang monumentally through the house,
the other people are little caricatures.
Raped women... she can be so badly damaged,
and abandoned by her family, and left with nothing,
but she can think, but she will flee,
even if she had had a family, and a sister to support her,
and the backing of someone, but then she would start to think,
but then she would flee, her Mega Piggy Family
and this family would pursue her,
to disempower her, to persecute her, to control her, to denounce her,
but then she would think, but she would never come back !

You people of today !
Your looks dazzling,
as if you don't take your word for it,
want to teach others,
and don't wear your hair down,
every city beneath you is drowned,
your faith on toilet paper,
no idea what you mean by "up there",
where you can't see anything through the fog,
everything revolves around your navel,
even your greed is immortalized on your face,
reveals itself as a living scar,
and the innocence of youth quickly fades away.
There is nothing, absolutely nothing,
that the public is into when it comes to mother's favorite,
as long as the damn time passes.

We see it's a wet summer this year. We had seemingly felt the weather. Since equally this day, that i gave my lawyer the report with documentation about just the last four weeks, and my witnessing friend underwrote that, she immediately called the landlord, and it was how i guessed, they have a special file for the sick one, with a number to reach any carer for her. She definitely got told a sharp word, because since tuesday i find peace here again, and can sleep. That made me relax and fall so deep in calm, that i was too tired the whole week, like others, too. Two days ago we went finally swimming again, in that time between wind and rain, and yesterday we walked outside in that time between wind and rain again. We seem to feel the bricks between, and nature is awesome happy for the water.

Back to the book, I've wandered between worlds enough to return to the meaning of diversity and to real life, stop crying and live. For fun... Moving to beautiful, green Brandenburg is about people getting in touch with each other and sharing beautiful, colorful customs, coming together across beautiful, colorful fields, just like connecting the variety of different people who come from elsewhere in the field. She nourishes unconditionally, moment to moment. To honor her, to love her, in infinite variety as far as our temple is concerned, your body is life. You are magic. Don't always apologize for the fire in you. Experience the stuff of diversity, walk through it, endure it or maintain style and wait. Anyone who no longer notices that woman's nature is diversity and that we all complement each other in tolerating this diversity is living without roots! Human diversity refers to the way in which a person learns to learn something from other people on their journey through life! Princesses have to own and condition all the idiots around them as much as they can in order to avoid limitless diversity. If you are jealous of the love of your country and hatred of the other, which you yourself represent, and you forego diversity, you are an idiot. Mental cripples see no diversity, but wish to shine in others, to impress others, in their need to be loved.

Money is a bottleneck, influence has a foreseeable end, power is on the brink, discipline is only for hoarding, pride is thematically derived, removed from change and resources, it hardly means happiness. Our claim is diversity, self-chosen action, a justified view of life !

We met a youngster couple by bike on the long cicle tour back home to France, that i just talked fluid french to them. Then came on the path through the woods a danish gentleman with paraplui very shy, like they are never talk a single word, i told him he should try those american wild berries, they taste delicious. Then some kindful joggers, and at least a whole open minded family with about five fire red hairy children, all so openly, the couple had adopted those many ones from their sister, she was not able to care for her kids. Uhh and again we talked out all things about red hairy kids, the envy of others, intelligence, and envy at school again, and a long tour through life as a teaching how to fight.

They got to know those french guys, too. And one elderly mom with her grandkid they wondered about a huge private place, I told there lives the police chief of town, and that i know them all as very kindful people.

Bye! Be welcome!
There is no such thing as bye.
Sentence with nothing.
It was probably nothing. Let it itch.
How can your perfect hearing
in its reproduction...
empathize with a foreign song?
Saz Evi, I'll build you a roof.
Four walls around it.
And also a room with walls,
and a hole in the floor,
I'll shit in there.
OH FINE !

My father, for his part...a so-called "angry, insulting rapist".

Now it's all clear to me.
He wasn't quite right in the head, just because he knew that crimes expire, domestic abuse cannot be proven, the rapes were carried out for him by others, into whose arms he just kept sending me, violence against the child cannot be proven, all close relatives denied the shame for him! HAHAHAHAHA, now it's all clear to me.
That's why, in addition to beatings, he always got this kick in front of the others without being punished. And when I was 14, I exposed him in front of others and laughed at him. That was THE reason to punish me a thousand times over for the insult, so I had been a dirty cunt to my father since I was 14, and even rape was no longer worth mentioning to him. I was not informed of the insulting things that had happened to the monster in his childhood or youth, but I was definitely informed that as a young man he acted out sadistic desires on animals, then the only thing he could do to me from afar was to denounce me when I was pregnant and steal the child from the confinement bed, and then at 14 to spoil and buy off my son with his lifelong lies about me and lots of money, which was worth 10,000 euros to him at the time. But my son knows that in the future he will no longer need money from bad people in exchange for their control!

Other friends who experienced the exact same familiar fatherly abuse, agree they had it the same. And that coward who is my father is still alive, he is 90 now, and i already have understood the whole thing, about his life long kicks. HAHAHAHAHA you see it is not a whole bunch of family, people would call this, and the German saying"Who laughs last, laughs the best !"

HOHOHOHOHOHOHOHOHOHOHO
A sadist may laugh just good feeling in laughter in his taking pleasure in attacking a defenseless child, but just as long as the truth came out ! then nowadays it is the pleasure on my side ! Once spread, the laughter is contagious.

Life cycle. Water cycle rotates regularly. The lover's worries.
The lover's doubt, Bird collar, Feast of the unknown village name,
The raw emotion of the new poet, The changing pace of civilization,
The growing aggressiveness of the machine.
On the pages of a book a farce of history awoke.
Why do you know the glass of water? How many fantasies floated.

If Americans, with sex and war films in the heads,
with eyes as big as plates, stand behind the curtain,
from where they see everything behind the veil,
as if everyone were standing on a plate,
from the edge of which the rest of the world simply falls away steeply,
people cannot bear the fact that reality
and having a real choice is out of the question,
until someone steals power with lies,
who simply takes away their cherished free world,
... in earlier times, didn't the Nazis also rob citizens of all free elections
through snake-like speech and seduction to violence?
people cannot bear the fact that women also marry for money alone,
plan for financial gain, and therefore get divorced,
if someone were to die under their roof, if a love of theirs left the house, if
an accident were to happen to a child, if someone were to take the mold out
of their hand, then one half of the offended people
could either become multiple rapists out of angry hurt,
and the other half could become hermits out of refusal to use violence,
but neither of them ever wanted to win over a new love,
because the picture of the old man would hang on the wall
and be framed there forever, and a large curtain would hang from it,
and not a new village would be founded, might soon bear its new name.
On a single large round plate, there is therefore no room
for a new beautiful village, in which love finds a home !

The fickle person, is he the one you can't count on?
The comfortable person, in keeping with his nature,
doesn't want any deviation. He sees being alone as a cold cave.
He compares being wet with isolation and being let down.
He prevents himself from perceiving wind on cool skin as a clear feeling.
He doesn't even breathe clean air and inhales cigar smoke.
He doesn't hold anyone's hand for fear of being hit.
He doesn't spontaneously meet strangers to give them his best gift.
He doesn't allow his partner to expose themselves in love.
He sees himself growing old and that makes him bitter.
He first judges others because someone stole his childhood.
He settles in places, but to avoid people there.
He doesn't trust the situation of being seen as a person of nature.
He doesn't tolerate a direct word, and simply demands humility from others.
He likes to share his discomfort, like when he talks about the weather. He
feels that the invitation of locals threatens his inner peace.
He gladly accepts any warning from the hater to protect himself.
He lets the people who feel close to his origins stand on the shore.
He goes into nature, but does not recognize himself as nature itself.

What did I always say? I don't want drugs. I don't want a boyfriend.
I don't want tits. I don't want to be a sexologist.
I don't want pubescent brothers. I don't want embarrassing situations.
I don't want to die in the sea of flirting, want no make friends for money.
I don't want a stage name at seventeen. I don't want to be an actress.
I don't want to perform a dance. I don't want a porn in a crochet bra.
I don't want a runway left at the end.
Who says that I need a counterpart to be whole?
Who says that I only want seven children by the time I'm seven?
Who says that I want to have everyone in bed for my career?
Who says that my friendship is a business plan?
Who says that I'll never see the little gray cloud?
Who says that the questions about my ideals are important to me?
Who says that I'm interested in the ideals of others?

Where is the runway? Surely you would know about it?
Would you know about yourself? Who can you stand, yourself?
Who would be able to stand him if not you?
If you look for yourself, you will find it,doesn't work the other way round !

You would... get the stars from the sky for me?
without getting me down from the tree? in broad daylight?
hahahaha and not knowing when the torrent would come and where from?
from above or while standing? really all sorts of things,
without your feet in the sand? into the stream, out of the lake
around my tent, away with the fairy?
should stretch my legs, your big fat toes?
and then eat salami on circular plates
with a bulbous glass full of Lambrusco wine?
I SAY NO! I SAY NO! I SAY NO! I SAY NO!

It's not a screw, my love it turns and swirls like water,
you flow here and back again, in circles around it,
like the tides, year in, year out, you change yourself and the world,
you are patient until spring comes, and everything starts again anew!

Hold on!
It's not ability in itself.
It's knowing what you can do.
It's said by those who know themselves.
It's believing in what you know.
It's not wasting words on it.
It's applying your ability !

Girls, don't worry, let the boy act as he pleases,
stood like that in front of me, also said,
because for years she had beaten him in the schoolyard, watered him
and I sent him to rowing, sauna, music
and self-defense.... "The Biggest Loser are you !"

As I understand it, that school bullies, too, whose pent-up aggression, including that of their mothers, can be directed at everything "else", even at the weird religious teachers, wouldn't bother me at all. They are also responsible for the desease of ..... the look-away mentality of all teachers. See who then "goes off" becomes terminally ill ! We can celebrate with nature, with friends who are real, and with our artistic skills that we are survivors of this time! Let us be proud that we also know how to heal, especially ourselves. I know the origin of my name, what others lack, as I have seen for a long time! So I'll stop now, make sure that you survive just like everyone else, dear friend.

ALWAYS STAY COOL! Or HOW MUCH DISCRIMINATION
DOES A HUMAN RIGHTS VIOLATION NEED?

Let's start from the beginning! When the bishop says with impunity
"Grow and multiply!" in the face of his abused altar boys.
When, in contrast to his chastity, the exact opposite is organized,
i.e. a secret swinger club, not with adults, but with children,
who are not even asked what they think about it,
the strange question arises, which a mother also asks,
whose child was once, quite selflessly and secretly
"stolen", "expropriated", in short "borrowed",
who would say like a child used for sex:
"It's nice to do something in a group for sex and to increase faith,
but it's no fun always being at the front!"

Shorts are not allowed in church. Weapons are not allowed in church.
But what if the same priests wear hot pants underneath, and the guns are
their dicks? But is a woman with mother's breasts, with a calm gait after
giving birth, airing the milk bar in public, whose guns ruin everything for a
woman?
                    WHO IS THE REAL PIG HERE?

29

Question: And what is the name of the one who likes them all? Buddha?
I just mean, from the moment I said the Lord's Prayer, I decided to run away
in a hurry, that was all it achieved. Don't panic. That's a good idea, I also
mean, from the moment I touched myself, I had 1000 moments of
enlightenment. Heaven for cats... oh, it's understandable, VERY
understandable, just imagine if they all thought the same orgasm out of
happiness, just the word, and then it all happened like thunder! Crazy, I can
put myself in a cat's shoes, they're all breathing technique artists.
Well, now I don't feel so alone in the world! Yes, the word is what scares
you. I wish you a good night!

Let me explain you Hamburger Platt ! After talking and say G'bye, guy said
instead of "Mach's gut !" he thought of "Hau rein !" that his Platt worked in
mind and he said "Mau ! Mau !" because we Nordic always say twice "Moin
Moin !" so why not "Mau ! Mau !" it is like "UNO !" and like "Schach
Matt !" this is a good way to say G'bye...! for explaining the wording
"Mau ! Mau !" always said the winner in a children Card game who won.

I'm going to turn myself into a herring, naked, halved, happily gutted,
breaded and fried in the pan, and wait until my tail stands up!
The reading of your friends new book is understandable. It is really a lovely
book, and the story for my senses and thought easy to follow. It is like here
the people who did not grow in the Plattdüttsch would only read and read
the wordings, then understand what is meant. So I have it with skandinavian
languages. Today I was making me sure, how far is my thought to a new
story to write as a story again, and I am content to slowly come to that point,
the basic thought are pretty clear, so I am balanced, and guarantee once this
year it will function. To paint a person just that is my problem, that i am not
aware himself and his face, what ever a laughing face is not easy, but my
theory is the issue of the painting the message and the background must be
funny. When the look on it must make you laugh a bit. It's how you see, you
teach and I will learn the impossible ! My theory you learned from both
sides, like i learned too, from that side that i did sport for many years in my
life, so today i am totally out of the game meant football, alcohol and

aggressivity, too do not want to walk out in the city in nights anymore, because those fools follow their neanderthal willing to find their kicks, this is for a woman, or even anyone who walked in nights outside in the black darkness alone to work or back home, like to see from each place you enter divide those both ways of possibility and better choose the right one, yes, but also see the good in it, that everybody always has the right to choose, you chose to become good at painting and you got it, and writing among other things. I chose to say, that i already know life, the people, the reactions, the dangers, and that long ways to solve problems with such, so keep the distance. Yes it might be the right way to see, friendship for both of us, might be the quiet best way to just keep the individual ideals for each one, and do the best out of it, that this is much worthier for us freaks and better not to try the love card, i would be afraid of it too much, to loose the trust once in just one wrong sentance spoken, and wupps all over, i am much too much overthinking. I am not willing to differ in someones blood, or become one heart for both, then i could not breathe anymore. Yes, for both of us, that is the normal way of living, it is better not to be infected by the normalty as usual, in order to better live in harmony and our own normalty. What is normal ? We are not normed to one. When we both have a normalty and balance found, then we are far better going with this, than behave in what the norm said in reality. What is real ? My life sense is not to belong to someone, like a pet, i may think critical hohoho. Let us stop here, or we find out the theory, why none would love none anymore, or why women would block the men, or no woman would bear any babies anymore. We must learn of each other, but it is not so risky like in a partnership when one single word causes death. Love cuts like a knife, and it kills, uhhhh no in reality most deaths caused by femizides in a relationship, like church said it, "We shall be bonded until death divides us!" I am not willing to marry a sharp knife. Sleep well, and may God bless You ! This is a good distance we use for cooling down and calming our emotions, feelings, and dreaming. This with you and me is more let the other calm down, more than having to dream always the same about a drowning world, and we do not panic. I know that you see the most films are real, you see the most dreams are reality. This is really good enough to be Good Friends ?!

31

Traffic light reacts - or traffic light governs?

Accompany an old lady to football with an umbrella?
Or in truth, like Lindner, not even set foot on Sylt anymore,
because of the punks living on the beach?
In 500 days, possibly politics, first the European Championship, 24 days
then 6 weeks of parliamentary summer break, 427 days left
then 3 state elections, results, accusations, 30 days less governing
Election in the USA in November - another 10 day break!
15th Dec - 12th Jan, and standstill in Germany 28 days
359 days left to govern, less 70 Sundays on which nothing happens
plus 10 public holidays, minus 4 bridging days, 275 days left to govern
7 months before an election election campaign, ungoverned,
so minus 214 days, statistical 15 days of illness and absence
minus 35 days of fruitless dispute in the government,
statistical government days 11, minus 1 day DFB final
minus 1 day Germany in the Champions League final
3 days for jet lag from summer time to winter time and back
5 days waiting for a broken government plane
If we are honest, the traffic light coalition
will have 1 DAY to govern until the federal election!
Bad luck if that is February 29th !

THE EARLY BIRD CATCHES THE WORM
Opportunity is the work of one's career.
Vanity like a wave of homesickness. I don't have to say hello.
Get rid of bad breath with a joint.
Get rid of the smell of carrion and your nose in the wind.
I don't have to fall in love. Feed the vultures and intimidate.
Keeping quiet and lip-reading is isolated silence. I won't forgive.
Describe the one from the front from behind too.
See themselves getting wet from the front.
The north as it lives.

Heike
Thieme

33

34

35

I only say "hello" to the one who meets me honestly in the morning.
Why does everyone always want..."the best part of the roast?"
or "the most beautiful thing is far away !" and then
"but you should be happy that the beautiful thing is far away !"
these are all just phrases
that are suitable for film titles,
but not for real life !

Never search for halluzinations,
do not follow the fools,
they invite for a desease lifelong,
but leave you stand outside the door,
you find the vision in your heart,
not a poison to consume gave that,
what you get is a nightmare,
what left you irritated and addicted,
what brings danger and suffering,
what grows the fear to believe in yourself,
what lets the other talk like brainwash,
what leaves the lonely wolve as abandoned,
what causes more searching,
and loosing your way to slow down,
and age coming earlier,
and physically get ill,
and loose all balance to heal !
The healing of every person,
is to be found exclusively in himself !

If the runaway is the way to survive, so why not ? If the tears of heaven
must be found back, you must find heaven.

I know someone who is living on the road. I have told him -

I notice that you're wandering around like a lone wolf, that can't feel so bad for someone like you! You're not a refugee, or in a caravan with the whole family. You just have to have fun, nibble, get drunk. You see them all, the others worry about each other, and you don't share this with anyone. You can hardly be perceived as someone who just gets what he wants. For you, there is only the moment. No plan for your tomorrow. No one waiting for you. No one longing for you. It's a bit strange, because you still seek closeness to people. It's also a bit believable when you hear people talk about how a life like this passes and suddenly people have been homeless for thirty years, as if that were normal. Then carry on living like that and be happy like a pug in oat straw! When you run into women you know, just in your thoughts, I imagine you see them all dancing in a row, scantily clad, along the forest path, and you sing from the bush behind them "Fox, you stole the goose, go after them!" or something like that... you'll be able to remember someone! Sleep well through the night of the full moon, and don't let yourself be stolen.

Oh, nooooo
to this day I have never imagined a guy like that,
as if his cock were hopping around, held behind a bush,
first the desire fades, then his smelly feet,
the lifelong fart that binds him, the salty sweat of lack of desire,
and only very lastly, the sight of the guy, and no desire at all.

Just imagine a bath that was too hot,
bright red ears in a towel, a stupid grin,
and he would brush his teeth, then introduce himself by name, ...
and show me a piece of nut chocolate that is stuck between his teeth,
because he knows that from his mom,
little boy doesn't go to bed without chocolate!

I walked naked a childhood long. That i won't love to kill.
I took distance to all who stole from me. That i won't drown mourning.
I took myself as value person. That sexually none had possession.
I first know emotion, feels, hate of others.
That made him think of a better solution.
I am from the woods. That i do know about good health.

None other would have taught me anything as long that nature medicine
would exist !

You could say the river flows backwards,
when the thin flood is pushed back by the bigger,
like people used to be locked up whether in the East or the West
for their free opinion and intelligence,
today there are still no walls,
children are locked up within the four walls.

PUMP UP THE JAM !
Supertraining starts in Mom's womb,
baby trains, moves, grows, walks through the cave,
forwards, backwards, turns back again,
not one single state, altime a change
has nothing to do about what romance feels
to later on be born as strong small fellow !

Love is not a show for superficial peacocks.
Love is not food for the bully for the grave of the unloved.
Love is fleeting like a cleaning product for those who cheat.

I learn non-violence. I love standing up alone.
Mother Nature teaches me. I insist on self-protection.
I am in a community.
I do not regret being loved.
I have a nice Sunday.
I am certainly attractive.
I have no loss in love.
I would be equal in emancipation.
I would recover from a distance without fear.
I would leave no doubt.
I advise no one.
I do not regret any decision.
I protect my freedom.
I sense my ancestors.
I work without stopping.
Fuck that cow Else who doubts this!

Today I saw, sitting in the middle of the high meadow
dragonfly, butterfly, deer and later on the path various eagles,
a young one of them white-headed the meadow hummed
loudly like seven motorcycles.

Which antiheroes, to put it mildly, "don't get your hands dirty?"
those who grow old, and are celebrated as "dignitaries"
in front of their followers, but are reluctant to admit
that they have to treat grown women, even their own daughter, like dirt,
and offer them every form of violence and prevent them from studying,
because they don't adore them? I didn't want to pay attention to the goings-
on at the fair, I didn't want to look like a drone over the weak and focus
my gaze on their fears, I worked for years to make the old people my
friends, everything is fine, just not everyone who pays attention to others,
because they condemn their silence.

I only celebrate with the CHOSEN ONES !

Sneaked away !
The family at the table, the table is long and empty,
the people are getting older, leaving, they are no longer here,
so often they have repelled themselves by me, all these years,
are no longer a strength of community spirit,
because they are all leaving, what they had in me,
was a guitar that was sold out, was a violin that was taken,
was a dandelion that was wilting, and I had cared for them for so long,
but from so far away today, I say, they can all be cared for,
I would even be the heir who sneaked away from the inheritance !

Imagine me so working as surgery, and one patient would die under my
hands, i would hang me up. Life and Death is so close but dramatically. I
love some people here in the close neighborhood, too. The more empathic
that people are, the more gets in vain when they must pass. AHHHHHH i
don't want to loose anyone, the one lady from a house aside, said, that this
appartment i live in, was the one of her old Aunt once, she worked 30 years
long in the archieve and she loves since beginning speaking with me about
the town from Middle Age until today. Yes, that is connected to my dreams
i always tell her, then she tells me the real historic background to it. I seem
to have a very clear view to past stories that really happened. Some other
elderly or people were born on one of our islands, they are lovely and feel
very much responsible for other people. But it is as people say important to
connect the history, and the dream to the third the real people, too. In my
grandparents house i found shelter, too, so that i was open to my world to
better understand by dreaming.

Strange, but that's how it's written !
It is often life savers who take your life again.
It is seducers who let you down again.
It is admirers who want to fuck you for their devotion.
It is the brothers without talents who are as replaceable as sneakers.
It is the hurt lovers who suffered financial pain when they split up.
It is violent supporters who are prepared to do anything for money.

But who was the murderer in the end?
It is recognizable as a pathologically narcissistic family,
that is where the perpetrator believes himself in most cases.

That's how it goes in families...the one,
with the empathetic something, with the looks,
with the skills, with the intellect,...is held up at the end,
well prepared and served ice cold,
to be served, to be dressed,
to be confirmed as confirmation of what the family
has thought up, so that they were ultimately "right"!

There are holes in the fence knowing I'll never to be the same again though
my garden death becomes me and sadness births lonely days never
permanent to sorrow me, it's only for a while until my sadness transitions
and I dandelion into a smiling face shines again.

That sounds lovely. I think like you do.
When that awareness of the own death,
holds maybe for one day, but you will watch someone's good eyes,
he is await, until you bear out back what is the sunshine from within,
it explodes upwards from heart, it shakes your heart, then sprinkles
the light energy into your tears, then might want your wings spread again,
you shiver of that erruption coming back,
and wanting suddenly laugh out again,
because life is such a paradoxy !

You caress my infinity that lasts beyond the flesh
my souls fire...how do reach through me
without touch...just the look in your eyes
the heat within, down my spine, teeth on edge...released my flow
trickle effect...spiraling beaded sweat...between the folds...
You have that same nature like me in you ! That sounds so lovely.
Selflove it's what prepares for such a moment not drown.

Regardless of his personal history of illness or past:

A worker's son meets up with his friends every evening
for milk drinks with synthetic drugs.

Driven by boredom, they go out, beat and rape, kick a homeless person,
push cars off the road, fight with gangs, break into luxury villas, assault the
owner's wife in front of his eyes, leaving a trail of devastation, both
physically and morally. When he kills a woman during a break-in one
evening, he is arrested. In prison, a new type of re-education therapy is used
to rehabilitate violent criminals. The treatment consists of showing films
about sex and violence. The sessions become nothing but torture. When he
is released after completing the radical therapy, his personality is broken and
he himself becomes a defenseless, manipulable victim of his environment...

this shows that any consent to violence, as well as violence against oneself,
never leads to a good end.

The way you walk naked, you are wondering about the eyes ?
The place you take a bath, you are guessing they want your hair ?
The distance from where they look, wanting you the hate to present,
it is the cowards bush, but always too late !
In your battle with the rest of the world
I advise you to side the rest of the world.

Going on foot,
secretful, directly, connecting
Trains .... light , fast, funny.

If you are such a crossing type, the kinda as i am the border type, always communicating with each one up to the edges, you are the spider and all will reach out for you in the center asit, like your mom came from the north and friends, and that musician from the east, and Mable from the south and me, maybe your one Dad from the east, the other one Dad from the west, the only closer type friends you have is two ones from the country side, and your working mates, north east south and west, how can you manage that ? I would take my legs and run, it is not an easy place to be. I could even not say, you might imagine me easier when make me a woman asit at the swedish border, what swedish border ? i mean there is only the Baltic sea ! i could not sit in the ocean to make you seeing me, to be a Swedish guy for it does not make it easier, you always have them all but they are far, i see you have it exactly like me, those i like are thousands of miles away in all four directions. Close yet far away. We are owning these characters of hawks, we are in thought speed at another place, so it is easy to understand the saying "You can blossom everywhere !" some fly more, the other get off speedy and won't come back anymore, the other ones stay in front of your window truly every day and daytime awaiting you. The birds family is HUGE ! but now i go off or i might become old and blind explaining all this !

People used to say: "Your wish is my desire!"
and "If your panty liner fits well, you'll never have to be afraid again !"
and for father's daughter, her wish will come true,...

but today we say, "One wish changes nothing,
one decision changes everything!"
that could be a signpost for everyone in the future!

No, people, rockers, birds, loners, ... for everyone!
don't fall down, get up, keep going, don't accept going round in the wheel,
because it has to be that way, don't assume that you have to
fall down, get up, keep going, because you become a 'hamster wheel'
from which you can never escape !
Decide ONCE

The small branch you are clinging to may have a thicker branch under the surface that you could sit on, but you have to look underneath first!
The knowledge of what is underneath will emerge after years of walking upright on its own !

When you consider how often the Russians
have attacked countries in the last ten years,
decimating the population, bombing everything,
and absorbing their raw materials,
Moscow is just the place for barbarians,
cyborgs and swamps, for someone like that the simple
church tower in the landscape is simply the tip of a
whale's harpoon that will impale him....!

The fine lady of society earns a good living by selling the children she is looking after to older men. The educator calls it the carrot and stick principle, for the participation or punishment of children by sadists.

Like fathers whose children they drill in an art of practice, no matter which one contains the black-pedagogical message, first you need to perform, then the art brings you pleasure.

And soon little girls are being advertised online, because of their loss of attention, admiration, affection and the prospect of easy money, even without school.

Eternal dependence with a broken will to serve until the end is the result of this. It has to do with shame.

See, hear, smell, taste, touch, think

the direct world of experience

mental phenomena - forms, sounds, odours, tastes, touches, thoughts, perceptions and feelings

beginningless, unimaginably, complex flow of causes and conditions

with mindfulness and clear comprehension the sense of ownership dissappears

who we are, our identity is not stable or reliable

the remarkable discovery can be both, exhilarating and frightening

practice, re-examine, re-cognize, with fresh unbiased eyes, we embark upon a quest to transcend all the ways in which we have limited and constricted our awareness.

The world is changing at a tremendous speed, all living beings are beginning to feel this, only narrow-minded people or those who deceive themselves and others continue to follow the same path.

You ask me if I remember you at times
I remember you when I smell roses
when i'm galloping horses
I recall your skin as i touch silk
&your eyes as i witness magic
Your hair comes into my vision
When I see a waterfall pouring
It reminds me of your emotions
as I see tides of oceans.

When i took off, my horse decided the way,
the horse took off in a hurry, the one joined his fun with me,
my little horse gave me free,
freed from the Planks, cell bars, boundary bars,
i fled in that vasteness a horse told me to,
so often, so fast, strong, proud, and stay where i am.

Be gentle as the highest credo, perhaps you are kinda too much of it. Better
than not, in real life, your are greatful, and right indeed, that gentleness is
the motor, that the believe in humanity, that the exchanges of love, and
careful get to know, it is. That's the way it is, when i do not care in every
single situation to share, then i loose the wonders of life ! It's just my
pleasure. Let it be so dear, water flows and finds its way. Take care !
Yes, the cherry blossom, the apple in the tree still grows !

Third-class, thin remaining...
applied for "better benefits" - Adapted women's labor law !
Women at work - not a German achievement!

Love is not a show for superficial peacocks.

Love is not food for the bully for the grave of the unloved.

Love is fleeting like cleaning products for those who cheat.

For the lifesaver, love is the fact that he takes your life again.

For the seducer, love is the same as being let down by him again.

Love is for the admirer, whose hurt over separation, whose devotion is only
sexual. But marriage is not a German achievement!

Love is for brothers without talents, who are as replaceable as sneakers.

46

For perpetrators of violence, love is the guarantee of support and assistance, protection only as long as they have made some kind of profit.

I am a woman who speaks her mind.
I am demanding when it comes to working.
I have a talent, so I was of no use at work.

As if I, as a German citizen who is not proud of it,
were described as "disabled" for my advantages. That saves confrontation and salary, I don't write on a machine that still allows Nazi keyboards to be used today, people like me insist on working rights. All I need is a Polish surname, and if I come out as "brain-deprived", then the workers - welfare would definitely have a job for me ! But anyone who comes with a semi-skilled social worker's certificate can always thumb their nose at me, even if they don't have any skills, they can and should live out their inflexibility in an authoritarian way, that's what is intended, anyone who does that has a job for life !

If the old love has long rusted,
the women stop coming,
it's like with the Chevy that isn't oiled,
everyone ends up an oldie, but not a goldie,
if he's not a civilian, always on drugs,
and under no circumstances can he just call himself Sammi, who opens the door and gate for him and then for the others,
the guy doesn't see much and has things to do,
no women jump on the threshold anymore,
not unusual remembering the drugged evenings full of ghosts,
"chaos" until you collapse, get it,
hold on, get away, unfortunate, first quickly over "red",
through the back entrance into the castle,
then "party in" together,
no question is accidental,
not to tell anyone what got into them....???

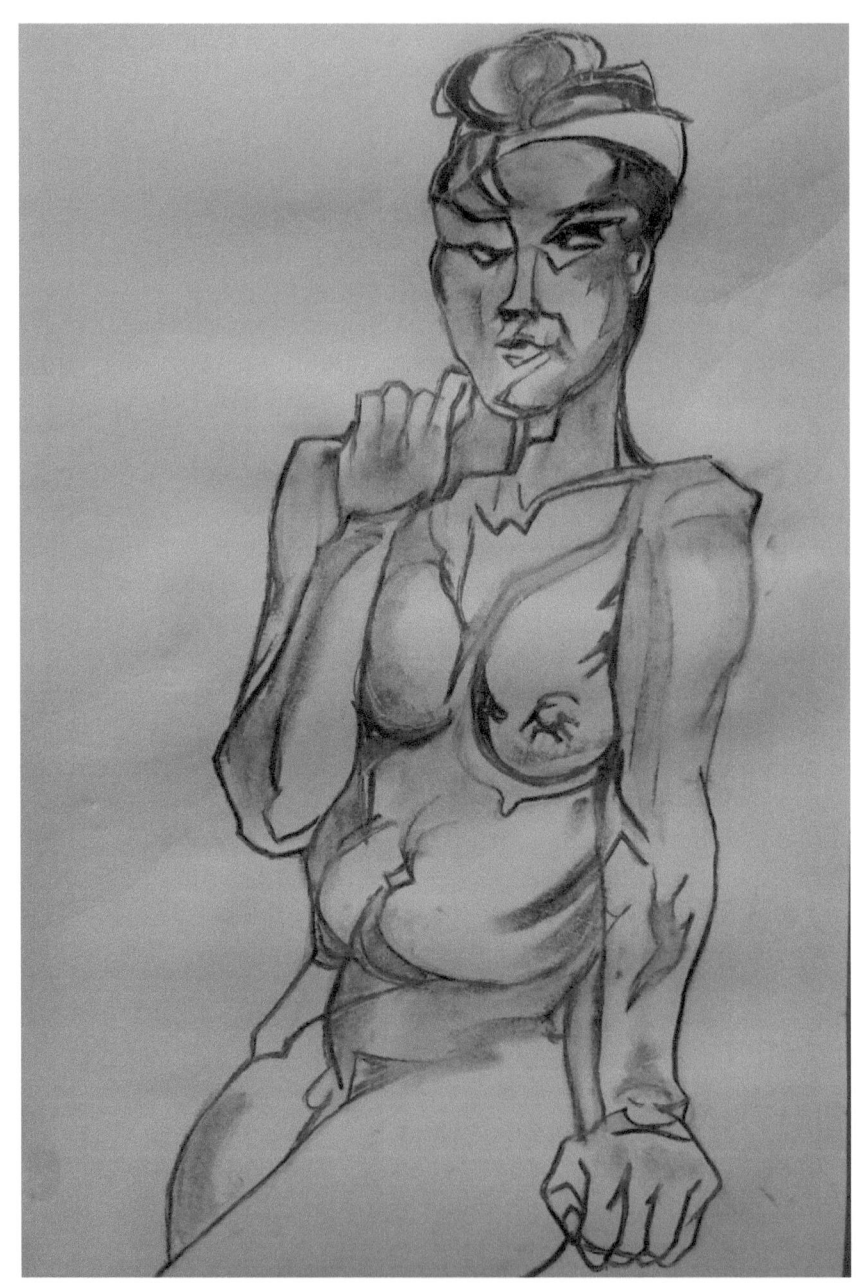

48

The Schleswig Castle Museum is spending at least 100 million Euro in state money and taxes to finance a megalomaniacally large metal glass reconstruction of the parking lot at the back of the museum. You won't be able to stop laughing at the end ! You see at the backdoor in this museum is a tiny door, from where those workmates from the museum sneaking in, those old ladies, with their old size beauty with their hanging titts and grey hair, soon become those sameway Bog body outfit of the one inside of it.

Symbiosis broken up, child theft one planet, the other next to it,
is not a wreath around motherly love, which is eaten away by worms,
the child is strong, very strong, as the patriarch wants to be.

Mother and child no longer exist, child gone, a skull on the back,
the creature feels powerful, the vow to harm,
the mother who does everything for her child, who only has distant tears
left, but they can flow very beautifully, the bleating howl of the sheep.

The life of two planets. The love of two estranged people.
Mother should feel guilty, she should drift in the sea as a drowning woman,
alone, like him in the world, of two planets. Fascists call the child theft
A STROKE OF GENIUS !
Let nature be your muse.
And not Women be the muse of the Fashist !

My life was not a straight line, was always gentle and smooth,
but help the beast in me, restless by day and by night,
followed the glance of the stars, the beast in me
had to learn to live with pain how to shelter from the rain,
and in the twinkling of the night might have to be restrained,
God help the beast in me, i told them "It was me."
It seems all so close, what they had seen in my cloths,
the small kid in me a teddy bear, that humor was vanished in the air,
of that was i was beware of the beast in me,
hadn't we unclear if it's New York or New Year !

It doesn't depend on the moon whether we lose weight by shitting !
It's not the soap that dissolves the fat inside us !
A few squats after eating would probably be enough.
It doesn't depend on the neighborly friendship initiation on the look
back over the shoulder that says, the other person has known for ten years
that you have been neighbors !

There are no patron saints in the church... for midwives,
who are hardly worth protecting for Catholics,
the business in their houses are more likely
to be caesarean sections performed in the district office,
none for plants and herbs, none for magicians, juggling chefs,
because the art is described as a lie,
and none for ordinary cleaning staff,
not even those who clean naked,
none for miracle pills for hyperactive people,
because Saint "Rita" hardly helps with ADHD,
none for that very special sausage !

It happens very rarely the fear is unfounded,
being afraid of the smell of a phantom's feet,
walking outside, socially phobic, but do feet smell?
I could even have stood barefoot on the coast of Genoa
at the age of seventeen, homeless,
but the sisters and brothers of the family,
who were planning their luxury holiday by ferry to Corsica,
were relieved when they finally
left the sight of me of poverty in Genoa behind them !

I mean, karaoke singing doesn't hold the record for continuous singing,
because glass noodles cooked far more widely, Asians prefer spicy soup,
failing to pass the driving test is not an issue,
not everyone drives a car anymore,
there is no need for a record holder for gutting fish,
firstly, there is hardly any season, secondly, weather phenomena,
thirdly, overfishing, fourthly, there is no tourism effect,
but because playing poker in the dark
is also widely frowned upon, this doesn't deserve a trophy !
The person who challenges usually has the choice of weapon,
whether it is a sword, pistol, bow and arrow, or axe.
Firearms are only allowed for a limited time.
It may take a particularly long time
to simply kill an animal in a nation of hunters.
That is why it is a state regulation in Canada.
But did the French still serve live songbirds with food in 1967?

The principle of underpants is understood very quickly,
why cover it up, what is so complex, who still wears them?
The underpants are boring as hell, connected to sourdough,
formulated with a warm heart to be wrong, documented by the artist,
certified as authentic, whoever exhibited this, my veto,
because my pants are not a museum for anyone !
Las Esposas, ... the loud ones!
Eating is at home, the marriage is concluded in the chest,
a person who belongs is someone who is viewed with distance,
cannot be defined at all, kept for worse times,
if the wife is good in the Tupperware chest,
most people are in the chest...lessness, if you like sex in handcuffs,
threaten to get your wife out, I also let my dog run around,
without warning him onomatopoeically that
he must walk at heel with me, the exhibition of the exposing woman,
waiting to see how well she would be appreciated.
THANKS FOR THE SWIMMING LESSONS!

In my opinion the competition is part of it, as are swimming lessons for children, because children first have to drink so much chlorinated water, spit it out again, and dive down again and again into the piss-filled pool, so that they never forget for the rest of their lives, because nothing makes you harder than drowning in dirt, what a piss mess it was that they learned to "swim" in !

Noodling is, as I see it, excessive hanging out by the pool,
with long legs, tight panties,
slightly puffed-up breasts, all lined up in a row,
for the purpose of showing the flesh to those who want to get married
and who never meet "real" women anywhere else in their lives,
due to time constraints or overwork.
These women are extremely sexually under-challenged,
as one assumes, which is why they like to noodle.
You can practically catch them from the pool with your bare hands,
unless they are thrashing swimming noodles!

We go to the water, reach in once, and catch the eel,
like the noodle of the sea, with our arm in the water,
because it is so easy to catch, the point of the matter,
whether someone goes swimming in the rain,
or doesn't, it doesn't matter !

She was taken from her family when she was a toddler and raised to be an unstoppable warrior. But for what purpose ?As Saku grows in power and begins to master the four elements - earth, wind, fire, and water - she'll seek answers to that all-important question. And she will learn that there is something beyond the elements - the Voids. If she can learn to bind the Voids, nothing can stop her.

Traveler on long journeys. Dependent on the outdoors. You are definitely not that. You show us the extraordinary fact that people still provide for themselves. You show how a man can manage on his own. You demonstrate the robust stamina of a trapper. You doubt yourself the least. This will be reflected in your psyche based on all the experiences and encounters you have had, enriched as a treasure trove of sun, wind, earth and smells. You are building up a human account that others dream of in romantic films. You have realized that the sunny side of life is unfortunately far too short and rare in a single human life. I firmly believe that you will not forget how to be among people! Of course you know that when you come back to the north you will always get a delicious meal from me, that is out of the question when you have something to report on everything that has happened in the meantime in the short time you are visiting, and on both sides. You see, I understand that your closeness to nature has become your ideal, and I will do my very best to avoid trying to take away from a friend what he has acquired with strong willpower; that is not done in the best of families!

Fitness for adults, woahahahah, with the fun factor, exercise is usually better, imagine the same as an Instagram social marketing doll in an advertising training outfit, with thick-rimmed black glasses that are supposed to look intelligent, and with a smartphone shining through the fitness club. I think that's pathetic. Sitting on the street with no clothes on, showing her pussy as if she were acting out the situation of underage street children, I can never think of a term for those who always post their entire everyday life on a continuous stream, what are they called again? They may be sick, but they still have a name that they are proud of, how sad. Influencer. Term for those who always post their entire everyday life on a continuous stream.

54

Wrong Brothers !
Against commerce, only butt-fuckery, fingers in the bum, Infantino,
we shouldn't kill football, we play naked and stretch ourselves out,
whether we're men or women, we show our balls,
don't give a number, every document says that we didn't stay friends,
to those who ask for money for a number, if a fraudster says to me,
I'm going to throw money into our relationship,
then that's not my club, and I say "no", don't go into the forest,
and listen to the screaming of those who just turn the corner,
and want to conquer art for themselves, get my rights for themselves,
cook up false names with the brothers, give women false slips of the tongue.

Enjoy the day! ohhh yessssssss after a hot, then cold shower, second pot of
coffee, and a bowl of pudding in the middle of the day, otherwise Saturday
is always a lazy day, my dog always gets annoyed by that because he's
bored, but the girl has a smoked pig's ear from the butcher before she goes
to bed, we've had really mixed weather this year, unpredictable, a week of
continuous rain at temperatures of 12 degrees, and the water for swimming
was like that.... then a week of collapsing into a coma in the extreme heat,
now it's time for cooling down again and a lot of wind, but we're grateful for
that, you can feel sorry for the old people, the constant irritating climate,
from autumn cold to Spanish desert sun, then constant rain with depressing
grey, and again wind that makes you fly away, hot, cold, hot, cold. I'm
young enough to say that it's exactly this irritating weather that makes it so
special, you stay young, that's how it is, the older we get, the less we age.

If I go to a... male doctor ONCE more, dude,
I'll hit Lukas on the doorstep, tell him how rape works,
throw him on his own mat, show him the boner,
sit down in front of him with my legs apart,
say, "I'm not here as a sick person!" I'm just here to "fire up the grill!"
I'm one of those really strong women, whose cerebellum
doesn't start to shrink at the sight of him, and I'd even...
"grab his balls!" can then find a male doctor himself.

Anyone who offers something to their children, goes their own way, takes responsibility for it, is of course also involved with heart and soul !
The thing of leaving a woman standing there without a word is like entering a museum, feeling at home, and then leaving the woman there like a dog, feeling free, and wanting to say goodbye, you shake the exhibitor's hand, thank the dog, he's there as a model, the main thing is that he's loyal and an unconditional friend, if you were to see each other again, a handshake, the woman's shell that suits her, her lemon-sour face, smiling in honor of it, and leaving her standing there, because no one could express it better than the wish after twenty years, for a happy, single life ! Simply treat the woman like a dog, smiling collectively, tying her up to the museum guard with a leash, and leaving her there, for amusement, that is the mentality – abuse !

Children don't look at the cloud
and associate it with the end of the world.
Children experience the sound of the sea
and call it just the sound of the earth.
Children feel good
and don't make plans for tomorrow.
Children experience enlightening moments
and consider this to be normal.
Children have to learn from a distance
and protect their own inner world.
Children don't categorize people
and judge them by age, weight and gender.
Children just want to be children
and don't experience places to make noise.
Children are swallowed by the wave of traffic
and the world worries about the paintwork of the car.
Children see their bare, round toes and don't plan for a high-heeled pump
and a pointy nose, wrinkled looks, mischievous glee, daily drinking,
the distinction between good and bad, following the ideal of an individual,
because thinking and forming one's own concepts
are too exhausting for others.

First portrait book almost abstract expressionism
unique cubist illustrations, provocative art
Anthology One: "For those who value nature!"
plus charcoal drawings and portraits
Anthology Two: "Portraits - Easter 2024" - - HEIKE THIEME - YLVA -

Everything used to be better,
do you remember what the sentence tells you,
think of my flute playing, another time I remember her
as a prostitute who didn't die, was burned,
and then lay in the grave, not everything was better then,
passing the test meant not drowning when drowning,
the music, the flute playing was lovely,
which the lovely maiden still enjoys today,
whether the witch lives, or whether she falls before everyone else.
Today everything is much better than it was then.
Today's youth are ungrateful. Today, think of a different time,
than "back then after the Cold War"; despite prosperity, work, and the booze
and booze, instead of having to freeze, you only had parents
who drove their children out of the stove in freezing cold, banished them.
In the past BURNED, today BANNED !
The mix of wodka orange or the none mixing, friends …
is today's like Mixing, ahh Mission Impossible !

Poor little mouse I was, escaped from the circus.
I almost died in the fray, won, and lost.
But I always had my BROTHER with me, who picked me up,
who gave me bread, who didn't run away.
He didn't have many words to say,
either he laid me flat or his face disappeared.
Because when everyone lied until the rafters bent,
they always came from the same nest, a poor little lonely abandoned
one like me wasn't offered the cherries from the trees,
only what fell for me in between, right?

Yesterday i met a funny aquaintance, you know this was a bit funny the last two years, i was appearing, i always was kindful and presented each one for a get to know one of my books, but the next time in the neurologisc corner a new young russian doctor, where i went. He made his view on my reception and awareness, and in the second meeting for my reciepe we had a colossal muscle fight about my warning to him, that i am not that type patient who lays down for him sothat he might get a jump for fun, and all what is my problem depended on a rape that was 45 years before, how i am aware of my own personality, and confronted my trauma enough of times, and may in future only heal myself, no othcr who did not come to be healed anyway, and i may dream in platttysk if he did not want to understand, and i dreamed of the kyrillic language in a secretful way, ... then he looked me directly in the eyes, said that he is not the slightest interested in that former doctor who gave me that diagnosis, that he is not take this seriously today anymore, and this fact does only exist for the file. Then we were quit, and he said, that i also may start to learn russian for him. Then i gave him my translation of my Art, philosophy and the reading of March into his language and two of my best books as bye bye presentation, and went to search me a local practice to get again usually my medicine from one single place.

Then again yesterday..... i had spoken to my new practice and a doctor she is loyal, competent, and was a chief doctor, now started here. She is overhvelmed of all what i did my whole life on my fight of life, and believed everything, sothat was the best way to get over a trauma, that is slowly passing. In this waiting room, same adress like my first doctor 25 years ago, when i sat an waited, had a nice talk to a lady aside me waiting. She began to open up totally, her familiar rapist story, the parental abuse, the Art she does, her physically trauma, the depression, and her woke head. That i spoke with her with a parallel knowledge, my Art i do, my best friend Carrie from Canada, and i took greatest fear from her. She really believed to be fucked by a socalled diagnosis that her brain was becoming smaller by time. I believe that is not true, it was a trick to calm her down. Now within our talk she could slightly arrive behind her own secret of life, and lost the fear to shrink in brain, women like her, that she and her thought is worth it.

So we see, it is every womans or mans special time in his or her life, when the day has come to live with the truth, but first you must have the strength to open up first, to understand the own life, does not mean another explained it to you. If it would be so easy then all could be read on a file of paper how to be healed and it would work, no there is no believe, that is only a weakness of some who follow their leaders, usually to be seen in puberty, but some won't take any step out of it.

Tell me, if you really thought, that any believe was found, i wrote and wrote in my books on 24.000 pages about all, healing, experience, learning, teaching, fantasy, creative painting, illustrating, warning knowlegde all types through all decades.... why would then not all those you call the socalled believers not buy my stoff, to heal with it ?? If people are weak, sick, traumatized, they live in their bubble, and the last they would do is read from a clear thinking mind, they are not ready for the truth and most will never be in this life. The youngsters will survive their crisis of puperty soon, but too those addicted to drugs in that strange time of building a brain, will possibly end in sickness a life long, and those people do miss school, work, success, love, selflove, strenght to stand up and fight. Those won't heal by any bible. It is reality, i know that's why i give the right book to the right moment to the right person as present, i can't open a book bakery, and present my 116 books like book reciepes, and then they came to eat my words. This is the secret of those who fought in life to find their truth, they will always find their way to their truth, when people fought for it, it is undestroyable. Nobody is playing God.

But the way to heal things out belongs to the right nourriture, and the moving the body. I had it like that, and it is a fact some short healing happen in seconds but the real way takes a life long. That is why i said that i may be chosen to heal, but the way that others won't be prepared for all of it, makes this risky to give too much of the power to people who would not be able to stand the whole thing to stand their own powers, that is better so to hold yourself back, the most responsibility a person has, is his own, no it is their ability to listen, the way they reflect brings them the path to understand and

59

find their own best solution. We are all just humans, with a lot of knowledge and wisdom since 50.000 years in our past of humanity, but we must look into ourselves to understand that, no body needs a leading, all truth is inside, all answers appear when wanted. The ones who don't listen are often the enemy to you, to others and themselves.

RECORD for the YEAR ! TWO MURDER ATTEMPTS in THREE PRIMARY SCHOOL CLASS ! MY COMMENT: NO COMMENT!
Rejected flirting is like being unable to deal with someone,
maybe it's also due to pushiness, jealousy and ignoring the fact
that Mr. Someone is actually in a relationship.

Hysterical morality and idealization is like turning a blind eye to the cruelty of your own children, and condescending aggression against your partner, who is blamed for everything.

Desperately holding the helm in your hand, is like thinking you're pedagogical, and teaching the whole world a lesson, no matter how brutally you ignore the fact that your marriage is in the shit.

Ambition to create a future for hyperactive children, no matter what it costs, to make others suffer, and to show off, to be treated heartlessly, instead of being celebrated and the talented child not being encouraged.

Stalking after the daughter, and spying on everyone, a snooping
that goes to the ceiling, to get rid of the school problem
and to shed the blame for the constant control of others,
when the child's career is finally secured.

The fear of failure, making something good out of agitation,
doubting the system, blaming the teaching staff, as if they and all their children were not fundamentally loved by the teaching staff, who themselves beat up others, torment them, look for the wrong role models.

There are holes in the fence. She escapes and vanishes.
Yet more borders remain. And not all are porous.

A dream of freefom in her heart. But the walls intervene.
She slips through the cracks. To face challenges unforeseen.

I saw her slip through, I looked at her, who was served on a tray,
sent off for rat poison, who was just declared a bouncy castle,
for a lot of fun calling "hello", who was only ignored
until she was persuaded to go for money.

I am sure that all lefties and conservative social democrates now will have
to join together to be warned of the Nazi time and Holocaust that was. They
want more attention now and will protest the right winged. We have to care
of our neighbors, and greet and not ignore only one of them. These cowards
all awaiting to break through every single brick they find in the walls. They
start with the young the most, in psychiatric hospitals, on lower schools, in
lost and abandoned zones, but truly forcibly in those scenes where people
feel "enlighted" and "elitary" to search for their follower promising the even
bigger enlightment if follow the leaders. If people loose now the contact to
the ground, and hide anxiously not to help people in need, and not give them
the needed solidarity, then i say "Good night". Because cowardly people
attack others unexpectedly, which the normal person does not expect.
Who, after fifty years of abstinence in marriage, no longer even knows what
sex is, and already says it in seven languages, still can't see his asshole, even
after forty years of defending his marriage.

Who, after a brazen approach to the fact of falling seriously in love for good
sex, out of the illusion of finally living, and exchanging nail filing,
nightwear, and separate beds for a piece of ass for the most beautiful asshole
in the world, still has dreams of cheating, and therefore swears on love to
run away.

So whoever thinks the most disreputable woman of all time is his angel and falls for it, that she wouldn't even touch him with pliers, if she could avoid it, and on the occasion she gets the gift of the year, all of his wife's stolen jewelry, the firm footing of the most stinkingly angry feet, learned to pull herself out of the mud, the fiercest cat of lost brothers, she'll break your neck.

Finding back to your own humor, is best medicine.
We did not stand our both feet stabil, in order to forget our own ideals, even the politic wants to lame the whole Europe and future of all.

Who knew that? That capers were simple tadpoles,
but when they saw soupy eyes, on the surface of a dead sea,
they were no longer comfortable being in the water,
so they got into the sauce on plates and the lunch of ordinary people.

Who knew that? That ferrets used to eat radishes,
until they were just round and fat, that's why they were caught too quickly,
and they no longer fit under cars, under which they walk in cities,
that's why they were left to graze in the fields.
Flying capers and round ferrets are also my favorite food, I catch them when
the moon is full, like today, make a nice béchamel sauce with them, and
make rice and meatballs out of the ferrets, the capers look at me contentedly
from the soup bowl, and then end up in my stomach.

How can you be called... Brigitte Hartmann?
That sounds in the room like the disgusting yuck Brigitte comes in...
she only loves herself, nobody wants to touch the sweaty one,
she is even disgusted with herself, my concern is the tapeworm'f childhood,
still haunts her today, because at least one guy wanted to get close to her,
but he preferred to leave her out of boredom,
then she takes a big shit on the toilet, she rid again, Hartmann,
whoever has ever touched her to date, Hartmann can count on five fingers !

See, under every shower another lady wanted,
when imagine the one, the other is hunted, waterfall is taken by the next,
in fact NOT YOU !

People are afraid of not being able to tell someone that they are afraid.
People fear the sky will fall if they don't say hello to someone because they
might not like them. People worry about hearing someone say in a tired,
deep voice over their morning coffee that the whole yoga thing had once
affected them in a more peripheral way. People can't allow themselves to be
the one they like and hold close to them. People may doubt that they should
leave someone as they are, that everyone has to carry their own burden.
People don't like to hear someone tell them about their trauma instead of
encouraging them to do just as well as you one day!

My lawyer lady and i phoned again....
and we both closed that case for the moment, because she also said, if that
sick one now registrated finally in her head to live as usual people do, we
may better not make her paranoid with the lawyers warning by landlord,
because that might end the opposite and she could really freak out again, but
in a way topped than before, i mean that is right, as i said it is good this
moment as it is, and i will call her back, when the torture starts all over
again. But that lady is informated, and she is still there, when i call her back.

Yes, my theory was that i catched her in the staircase once she was a real
freak that time, and she stood right in front of me with one of her people or
carers she had, sothat i said it to both, that her terror of nine years long
might have to stop now, or she will hear from me !

Yes, and the other point was, that one guy who really passed bye a few of
times, and once slept here as guest, witnessing, that he did sit on my couch
that morning with his coffee in his hands, and started with his male deep
voice talking suddenly loud enough that early that one from up could notice
there is a man in my place ! From that day on she held peace. Was maybe
the right trigger for her.

63

64

Yes, it is a fact that real sick ones like that chick needed different other triggers, as usual people do, it is not the spoken word she changes behaviour. We humans are connected in another way too, that is the sense or the vibes, or tendency, or tension. Yes, my dog is in me, round me and surely gets nervous when something destroys our both peace.

Guys, isn't it good to be a social mature being ?
you know what to do in every situation
you know where to get the help you need
you know who is protecting you
you know to be aware of what are your strenghs
you have the courage, wisdom and strength to strive
no matter what today sends my way !!! Now i have stoff on 85 pages,
so now from that moment the story is just fun, like painting, you first collect thought a while, then soon feel a connected idea, then looking around and see the real story around you and compare to build chapters, then collect all those new sizes of people you learned about, and that all gets enough then the story to connect and tell a little around those things is just for fun, first you have the work in collecting weeks before, a real book will never be written without the contact to other people. It shows directly the neighborhood of mine, the typical people in germany i met, the passing of the past, my stand up in life, those many many characters i see through wether woman or man, and shows it from the real side of character, now it is in the start to try to fold out any story maybe, but could be a reality view again, or the use of real weirdo characters of people who build a story.

WINDOW GLASS BUILDING BLOCK
It is something very big, it eats as much as it can,
it pops into the toilet to flush out what needs to be done,
the stream sheds leaves and makes noise,
the lame snail peeks around the corner,
it sticks out very sluggishly from behind the bush,
it scolds, discriminates, devalues the encounter,
it eats at mother's, it avoids looking behind the window glass,

In this case I would only recommend trying it the old-fashioned way,
and better leaving the thick glasses inside,
because you can't see the neighbors through bulletproof glass!

A dragon who liked to breathe fire,
spotted a female dragon
and he fell in love with her.
She moved into his dragon's den.
The dragon kissed her passionately,
with fire from his lungs,
the dragon lady was sweating
and had blisters on her tongue.

Alfons Pillach

Until we have made peace with our own
death and accepted it, fears will always determine our lives.
Love is the joy of life that knows no age.

The love of two estranged people.
Mothers should feel guilty, should drown in the sea,
alone in the world, 2 planets, fascists
call child abduction a stroke of genius!
Let nature be your muse. I was shocked
at how many young women's children are denounced and stolen at birth !

Spoils of a booming economy,
all the wealth & money never down to the teeming millions
- the toiling minions gravity doesn't hold as fortune trickles upward,
that's how society's structured - an elite scheme, equity is always a dream.

PAIRS DELUSION
MANIAC BORDEDOM
UNHAPPY LOVERS
DISFUNCTIONAL SYSTEM
WEAKNESS IN UNIVERSUM
SHARED LOVE IN TWO
DIVIDED LIVES and HAPPINESS
SLAVES IN AN INTELLECTUALITY
SHUT THE FUCK UP and DIVORCE !!!!

To the locals, the hardcore softies,
those who sweat blood and water in every encounter,
who sniff and trim themselves, who can't help but constantly have to watch
how... the secret of the river is revealed, that it must always flow
DOWNHILL! LET IT BE TOLD YOU!

I saw a single walking mother today with her baby in her cart, she seemed to
be of an age a little too young to be a mother, so about 18 years old, and she
was fat like a hippo, and when I saw her again later, she was walking up the
soft path for about 100m, she was almost hanging on the ground and
couldn't push her cart, she looked like an old person who couldn't move or
breathe anymore. That is sad. This is more the tip from me not searching for
yourself, Be yourself ! Can you differenciate between the experience, after
have had the dinner ?

Mr. So-and-so, be careful, you can fight me, that is well known,
but I propose a solution, you will not forget it !
There were fathers who used to pay a lot to lock up children so that they
would have a serious diagnosis and their private lives would become
socially nonexistent. My father was one of them,
but in 1982 the laws changed, I just had to escape from him,
TO THE ASS OF THE WORLD, in other words to the north,
and he no longer had that means, my lawyer told me, only to never return,
what a stupid coincidence !

Thanks for the tip, first you get taught about assault
in the family, and deprivation of liberty, then you run away, have a child,
and the slanderers again classify the child as assault
at the time of birth, and deprivation of liberty,
then see how you are left alone as a deer,
that feels and has to experience being alone with it!
Thanks, now I know, how that feels!

Lovely ain't ? Am not lazy while i would stand
under the showering waterfall just awaiting that "Love" to the next,
from the last, to the next one in my chain, even without a word,
i am not myself one of them who stand for an illusion, in no silent willing
to be loved, i am not to be changed like a perl in the chain of all others !
A woman is not the towel from each cheap motel to get,
and consumed like a warm summer rain, fantastic and Big Thanxxx to you,
my friend, i know i am aware of my wording, that from some time to time,
those words are shared, and people missunderstand, this is our fate to get to
know the people even it takes some years, to find the trust in someone !
and for your info the best and powerful shamans teach me to be bold to
write their thought on my body to protest and be uncomfortable and show
my anger every single day !

I know what you mean, that i am sameway angry just about the fact, that
there is fight, i would have broken my own bones, in order to tell them to
stop with it. To try hard to get past the anger part, it's like you say, the same
doing since i am on earth my heart lets me pass over, i know, but the mass of
remember causes it takes years. I know it's no solution, to react powerful in
any cases, not to suicide, and sameway not to become aggressor, it's like you
said it, the best way to find things out, in silence with yourself, and find the
strength to strive.

Everyone does that !

A child doesn't fall off a church tower, when it has its first friends,
a child hardly loses its mind, if it tries its first joint,
a child becomes an adult, when it goes on its first half-world tour,
a child blossoms, when it has friends all over the world,
a child doesn't have to take its own life, if it has been in love a few times,
a child is no one's property, so it chooses its true family !

THE KILLER ARGUMENT !
The whole it's "my child", it's "my home"
only leads helicopter mothers
even when they object or distance themselves
to chase "the child" out of the family FOREVER!
First they have their feet at the table, then they have no place there,
they should rather not have to learn anything about the truth
about history, secrets, antics, that the beatings when they resist
only serve the "well-intentioned upbringing",
that the healthy sense of humor
only serves the "supposedly sought-after" spouse,
and the family career that has finally been achieved,
if at all, according to the registry "office" what else are daughters for?

France is stumbling a little. Corona, right-wing politics
little in the fridge, no medicine for the poor
provision for births in decline, state medicine disastrous
staff shortages, no pay rises, poorly paid doctors are emigrating
protest movements, racism as mainstream, environmental pollution......
If the Social Democrats win on Sunday,
negotiations will begin very quickly
to improve the situation in the country again,
otherwise, deterioration is guaranteed !

With the brain damage, the lack of empathy, the lack of insight,
the dependence on the ego, the fear of letting go,
the shame of making mistakes, the distraction from noise,
the lack of positive thinking, the withdrawal from people,
the resistance to the world, the loneliness of living alone,
the accompaniment of all knowledge within me. I endure patiently, and one
moment silence, which runs over me as pleasantly as my skin, has been like
this for a long time and it doesn't need to be more than that !

What America ?
If the American flag offends people, the Americans should get out of their
countries. Cool said, indeed. And what about searching afterwards for that
One Tree with the Free Wind in the Branch ?? I only speak about the loss of
Elvis Presley, and Marilyn Monroe, in former days, the Hippy Movement
was healthier than the basic medical Treatments in America, and i forgot ....
the existing high standard medicine for specialist still for the upper class
indeed against a few more bucks. It will be a Win and Loose in future.

Oh, never mind, it's like eating spaghetti, how the woman offers me
to make millions if I include the crazy wave
behind her at sea as an investment, first pay in 300,000, then she promises
to make a guaranteed profit with all my audio books!

Eating spaghetti is like, without any liquor, know that
if you drink 1 liter of my piss, you're guaranteed to get healthy,
costs only 400 euros!

Eating spaghetti is also like, according to a compliment,
I should write well, so I should quickly write 1000 euros,
and I'm guaranteed to get 45 books for it!

Eating spaghetti is also like giving a sugar daddy his newborn orphan and
doing anything for his $20 bill. Eating spaghetti sounds like believing a
false document, let's go on a journey, love, and see how friendship pays off?

Favorite sentence in a joint collection of bankrupt banks
"Are you all crazy?" now the tails have been artfully placed on the roofs
financed from red numbers and you still want to admit, over your caviar
breakfast, that you didn't want all of this?!"

"I think of those, who were all known in Israel in 1982,
while traveling through the country, I ask myself how in times of peace,
since a dictator has been massacring, ostracizing, inciting people
who are a little different for 20 years, and now even wants to exterminate
them, using the term "land grab" to dryly carry out a genocide on a tiny
country bumpkin that had no precedent, I think, how many of my friends
from back then, regardless of their origins or color, could still be alive
today?"

What do I get for 5k Euros?
Let me think of it.... 1 k Salt ? I know Salt is not easy to get.
Purchasing power, low wages, little work, despite a shortage of medical
personnel but most of the deficit is with the people themselves, whose
health suffers from malnutrition, which can also be traced back to the lack
of food and products on their shelves! If you talk to everybody in Great
Britain, you do not walk behind the truth, you do not stay behind the curtain,
you understand their strong willing to live healthier, but can't reach the
products, those who keep health. I know that people confront truth,
and think other places are different, the sell is the own cheap products, in
order to keep the people filled with sugar and fat, as expensive as wants,
those farmers all go plead with that, the sick consumers have no choice, the
sicker they become, the more they need it as sugar and fat addicted, and die
earlier, because at last the sugar fat addiction is far worser than the alcohol
addiction, sure kills slower but harder. Ah i see, translation problem, i meant
- What do I get for 5kg of euros? Let me think... people talk about nature
salt, that product keeping the health, instead of industrial salt, that is pretty
much unhealthy. And the farmers can't sell their products to fair price, these
farmers are going bankrupt.

My "deflowering" was inspired
by the question of whether I and the amphibian, the sow,
whose wife I was probably drinking this drink together with him,
it seemed so blue, he actually drank it, I didn't, so I was the amphibian
who got through, what a pity about the man !

Mojave Desert ! Sonny Barger made them upset,
they had to talk about it, the topic about driving license,
they had to keep the principles of law indeed,
was a faking bad and humorless, better turned from Angel zu Hell,
not needed the Witnesses for anything,
so no Jehova at all, who lived in a slot
as high as the cloud to wait for Jesus came,
in the Lower East Side both were concurrence,
but at least it was God who Personal use announced,
who kicked them out, needed no Jesus until today,
who ever had the longest way to cruise
but made the fault drive a japanese motorbike
way up the hills, in the Mojave desert ?

Who orders that future married couples first have to complete a six-month
probationary period? In the modern 18th century, corporal punishment in
marriage was no longer common, even if it was still punishable by death,
at least the forced imposition of the woman was still common, and then
violence was also used if she was unwilling, the woman's cohabitation was
finally compulsory, if she was unwilling the woman could be locked up, and
only the wealthy son-in-law was allowed, the divorce was only made easier
for courtship, and the virgin tax was a must! All of this seemed good enough
for the young people to plan a little more for their future together.

Denmark or the North, yes, sayings wordings, but that familiar
neighborhood makes it teach us many things, it is our languages have much
common, this is altime the difference of the region where the words spoken,
the region always variates the meaning, there might be so many

interpretations of meanings like people living in the north. That doesn't sound like similar languages, no this is a nordic way to see life, so the region colors our speech, every little difference in the spoken words, but the same meaning, i explain that different people have different backgrounds to speak the same wording, and the region the weather and seasons change, the age of a person, the life lived, the intellectual ability, the ones who speak lesser or are big tellers. The more tolerant we see the other person speak to us, the more we understand each other, this depends not on how much we speak or how we are dressed, some people are often understood by recieve their smile. To talk to people like that more, i would love to, but i am not rich enough to go on travel, and i am not able to pay that price to walk and wander around with my backpack and dog, and sleep outside like a viking, because my nature is not strong enough for this, to get to know all the lands and people, yes, we are not on the run, but that is good, those who are travelling pay the price of being more lonely because the have still the hardships to survive and be responsble for it alone.

The English do the same. The North to them is that which lies between London and Scotland. ? yes, isn't it funny ??? this is a cute world sight, a different universe in many others ! They also think Hadrian's Wall is the border. Quite bizarre since the entirety of it lies completely within England. I haven't seen it. But my trip to England stopped right after i landed when at that night the officers did not allow to enter without money or any adress, and i think i had no papers, too. We have such a small viking wall here too, the wall that once defended the viking from all the southern wanderer who came for business. It is called the Dannewerk wall. So when the vikings travelled around, they always brought a little wall with them to feel safe and think of home. nah, that looks in our landscape more like a dam, you may walk on it a while between small trees, and fields to the left and fields to the right, that wall was more i think a symbol, that dam and the wall was used to stop the traveller waves, i think to make them business here at place. We have stones from the GDR wall ! We better do not discuss how many walls we had to have around us.

Should I publish satirical newspaper articles?
Can I walk people's dogs?
Perhaps I could also write eulogies for those affected?
I would also sell apples for all I cared? I also played billiards and cards.
Philosophers and poets like me have the least
opportunity to participate in earning money !

If I still try today to justify myself, not to digress into old bad behavior,
like drinking, traveling, gossiping, I would also have the reprehensibleness
of speaking rudely to an official outside, even from behind is standing,"No!"
I immediately say like a shot, "I wouldn't dream of it, I went to the fire
hydrant before, which was less bothered by me urinating !"

In 700 AD, the Welsh were recognizable as soldiers by the fact
that they had the leek on their clothing,
men without leeks had not dived,
it was the time of leek signals, instead of smoke signals,
there were 200-300 million people at the time,
the Arabs invented soap, by combining oil and lye,
burping was the WhatsApp of antiquity,
imitating animal noises does not fit in the city.
At that time, someone had married
the Berlin Wall in memory of the Berlin Wall,
in order to gain recognition in the village, any means were acceptable,
but then at some point the marriage fell apart !

Dr. Pepper (est. 1885) feeling better cont'd their public
domain quietly beneath Walt Whitman's #vss365, 52:

I bequeath myself to the dirt to grow from the grass I love;
if you want me again look for me under your boot-soles.

I stop somewhere waiting for you.

My first run through this story, was my escape from the family,
I was forced to eat their filth, which I did voluntarily, until the day when
I got up again with my beloved grass, and flew somewhere else,
the flight was strange and long, in fact and very strangely I had landed,
but I arrived in my own life !

EVERYONE'S CONSENT means they take RESPONSIBILITY for it!
EVERY CHILD with a strong will knows that the SEDUCTOR
has been designed to their DETRIMENT! Otherwise, THE INTERNET will
be to EVERYONE'S GREATEST POSSIBLE DETRIMENT!
Yes, I know, we humans are ALL ONE FAMILY, whoever goes under by
submitting to American IT companies, also commits political death by
agreeing to prostitution, he is cheating them ALL together!

In the same way, as the woman cleverly offers
to make millions, whoever translates the insane wave of the sea
as "more" for the sake of greed, and includes it as an investment
can only pay in 300,000, then the AI promises
to make "0" profit with all audio books guaranteed

How to eat without liquor, know that if you drink 1 liter of his piss, you
promise to live healthily, only costs 400 euros up front, because for the sake
of the specialness, everyone claims the right to make candy out of shit!
Eating spaghetti is also a way of attributing talent to everyone, but
friendship is also supposed to pay off, so according to the compliment you
should pay good sums for it, as soon as possible, that is supposed to give
you potential! Sugar Daddy is a perverted child molester, he shows his often
newborn orphans what they lacked in "love" in life, and uses minors to
make up for his crappy private life by doing everything for him for his 20
dollar bill. Eating spaghetti sounds like, believing a false document, let's go
on a hike, love... but don't get lost in the forest of admirers, yes-men,
recognition, affection, partnership, compliments, solidarity seekers,
coaching FOREST, and see how friendship only pays off for absolutely
nonexistent people or AI systems?

Have you ever tasted it?
Ohh i find the very good Nothing tastes even better than Shit !
Yes, the Shit to eat, meant also the very same you eat,
a month long from one pott. I know the right one, is quiet the one, who eats
from golden spoon, then tells you "hello" by "you don't belong to me !"
then runs out the doors and with blown cheek
he she it spits the child in front on its mouth even with
the "Eis am Stiel !" that costed MUCH SYMPATHY !!!
Not in our coastal waters, rivers and drinking water anyway. I know the
small stubby middle class performer is not seen as german monument
anymore, ... these times passed. That's a fact. But caused not a momument !

Sometimes I think like this
you don't want to offer any service,
the whole hall is full of flatterers,
get them drunk, all the hypocrites,
just come because there's something for free,
the hot chick doesn't want to have to get married,
I left the cold plate standing,
I punched the bear in the chin,
I left the bedsheet clean,
it drives past, the sex limousine,
the high voice of the "Oh, God screamer - goodbye!"
very modest as I see it,
the child born from it, no cheese soufflé,
no wholemeal bread for the lunch break,
no command for the handmade little housework,
no tolerance for the small dick,
it would seem like a waste of time to me,
no need to marry the one who just swiped.

I no longer regret attacking a horse from behind,
but only doubt that it will kick out the back of my head !

I no longer sing to stand out among the crowd,
but rather just happily walk past them !

I no longer drink to summon the ancient spirits,
but rather to not stop laughing at the spirits of today !

I can no longer bear to remember the effect of this,
through a constellation of parents who managed to not speak a word
to each other their whole lives.

I am afraid that I will no longer be able to claim that I have found
the best conversation partner in every animal I have met !

I only decide who I find to be an asshole as a friend,
and not which assholes would like to know me in the future!

I do not study the people who leave behind a bar feeling
in the family circle that can no longer be distinguished
from smoke, murmuring and quarrelling.

I had one first painting book too, did you get this one too ? Some of those
paintings are in both, the size is a tip smaller, but more paintings, yes, now
this proved us, never stop dreaming, never end in a day when there is no
inspiration, once there will come a day, and somcone will be happy about
that ! The first, it was done for a very good friend Kali, he did not talk to me
the whole damn life long, but he spoke on the phone for half a year long
about his damn long life., and who is damn sick physically, when his
partnership was in crisis, we spoke and shared our both Art half a year long
intensively, so this book was dedicated to him, he got it to his 55 th
birthday ! this first edition was a kinda show of my dreams. The second was
kinda try to teach me in portrait coal painting.

78

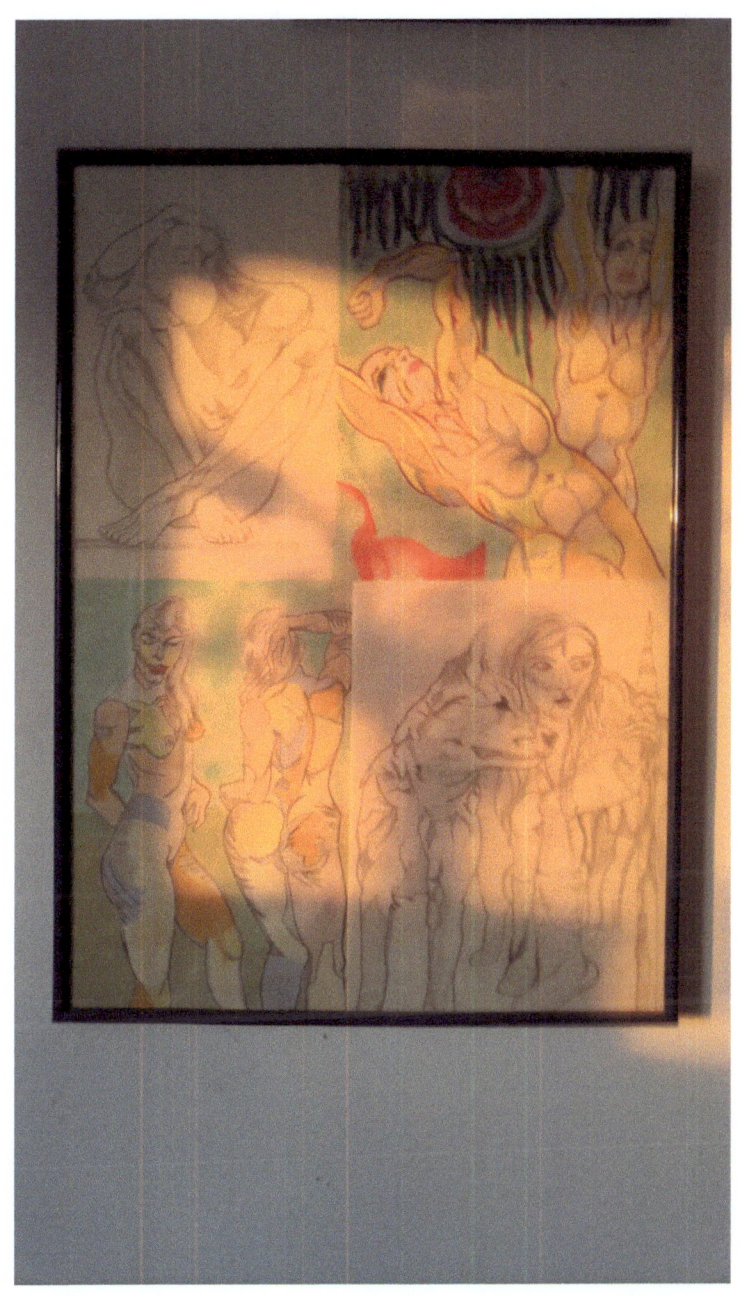

80

England has a good political front to the old right winged Tory, the social democrates won. Poland did the last time the very same !

Let's see how France will function Sunday, Yes, it will be much interesting ! Indeed i remember the French as very proud on national culture things, the theater, the tourism in the areas with high cooking tradition, they love their landscape, but still ignorant what depends on nature protecting, and nuclear power, and they love to present themselves like higher being to all other countries, they do not talk with anyone who is not owning their language skills, sothen they won't feed you. Yes, when they will become nazi, they will loose the whole rest of reputation as holiday land, and loose their tourism, too, yesss, then they might loose that famous french title in their contract of France "Liberté Égalité Fraternité" like "Freiheit, Gleichheit, Brüderlichkeit" this might end and they might sink into the title "Nazi, Fiends, Military", the people vote, the people get what they are friend too, yesss, indeed because the East Nazi Russia and China works steadily to divide each country before every single election, now imagine it is a fact that USA stands at the same abyss like France.

I have that those mornings when i had a night with relax, and had made a round about the last time and fell in deepness, then those mornings my body does start a let go parallel and i shit once after another time, you see our body is our best friend, so tight to how we feel, he is like our dog, he reacts on how we think or let go.

Walking the dog. Then on the way back she jumped into the little swamp and had a little bath then she got better and I told some asshole on my way back not to point his long arm up to the sky (like a Nazi) with his child in his arms because it was scary for Mable so he had to stop doing that kind of thing, my dog didn't think it was funny, she didn't want to pass the guy who looked like an elitist eco-shithead, he apologized and let us pass, that was finally something, in fact if that happens to him again I'll just raise my voice a little, whatever, you know I never ignore it, I taught him how to behave. It's the rich who need to be taught how to behave, how weird that sounds, yea, and give them a kick, they can have and own and get what they want as

if everything that is grown is their garden of paradise. I always think of the elitist, tall, asshole father with wrinkles and grey hair who gave birth to a son and who, like the typical psychopath, thinks he's so damned the center of the world that he never noticed the womb the boy came out of, as if the boy thought he gave birth to him himself hahahahahaha, the clone gave birth to the clone, then why the mother's womb? This fact is why psychopaths never talk to their wives, they ignore each other. Yes, he thinks to himself, "It must have hurt to give birth... why can't I remember?"
This joke was insightful.

A liar uses strange parenting methods
to show the child how easy it is to lie, while still putting on a neutral face.
A liar puts friendship above correct behavior, will describe the cucumber as climbing material, which doesn't grow as well as his lies.
A liar sells you a Ferrari, and lets the discount fly across the room,
without you ever wanting to buy it.
A liar confirms when he says no, and uses sex to make amends,
even if he says his own wife is dead.
A liar would never mourn honestly, his emotional structure would collapse,
so he would continue to lie, because everything is fine.
A liar knows that he needs people who, out of gratitude for attention, for his clever alibi believe him in all situations, even when he lies to them the most.
A liar regards every single person as a leftover good-for-nothing
who lacks a sense of reality, so that even the second Jehovah's Witness
must have run away from him.
A liar doesn't like going to work, he sees all of his colleagues as idiots
bathed in innocence who lack marital sex.
Liars are most likely to look for their alibis in dingy dives, where the blonde wallflower, the pining single mother, or the excluded colleague,
who he thinks is broken enough to serve as a garbage can,
the liar thinks loyal friendship is something that only those who take themselves too seriously fall for, let them talk, he is prevented from lying.
Liars fall for themselves where they are trusted, walk up close to them,
you can feel it because the lie becomes infinitely thicker.

Liars do everything they can to appear credible,
that's why they send their signals to other liars, the worse the others,
the better he looks, and where the liar places himself, no grass grows.
Liars often claim to be very normal people, in marriage it was normal to
argue now and then, because someone
who is deeply involved in lying has to appear normal.
Liars appeal to people who believe in the illusion of love,
who believe that happiness must be something you can climb to,
because if you believe deeply you don't ask for the truth.

Why do the best women always believe the lie that
the most important thing among friends
is to say that the right man is only one of those
who told the woman in words that they loved her,
and that is precisely why all women fall for all men !
Instead, women should learn and understand that
it is not a question of being told that you are loved,
but rather of seeing that this does not happen,
it was always those who were responsible for botched love affairs
that said that she simply did not deserve love !

My good advice - never get married!

Never let your husband......out of your sight,
or he will have dug a hole,
and left everything behind for a climbing cucumber!
It would have been nice if it had been that way,
that about before, that about the lie, Vauvenargues once said
that it was always good to talk about something
again that had already been discussed, so that what someone had said
about you or your mother only applied to a love-hungry, unbeatably naive,
obedient receptionist in the foyer, who was supposed to be saddled
with all the sick and disturbed people.

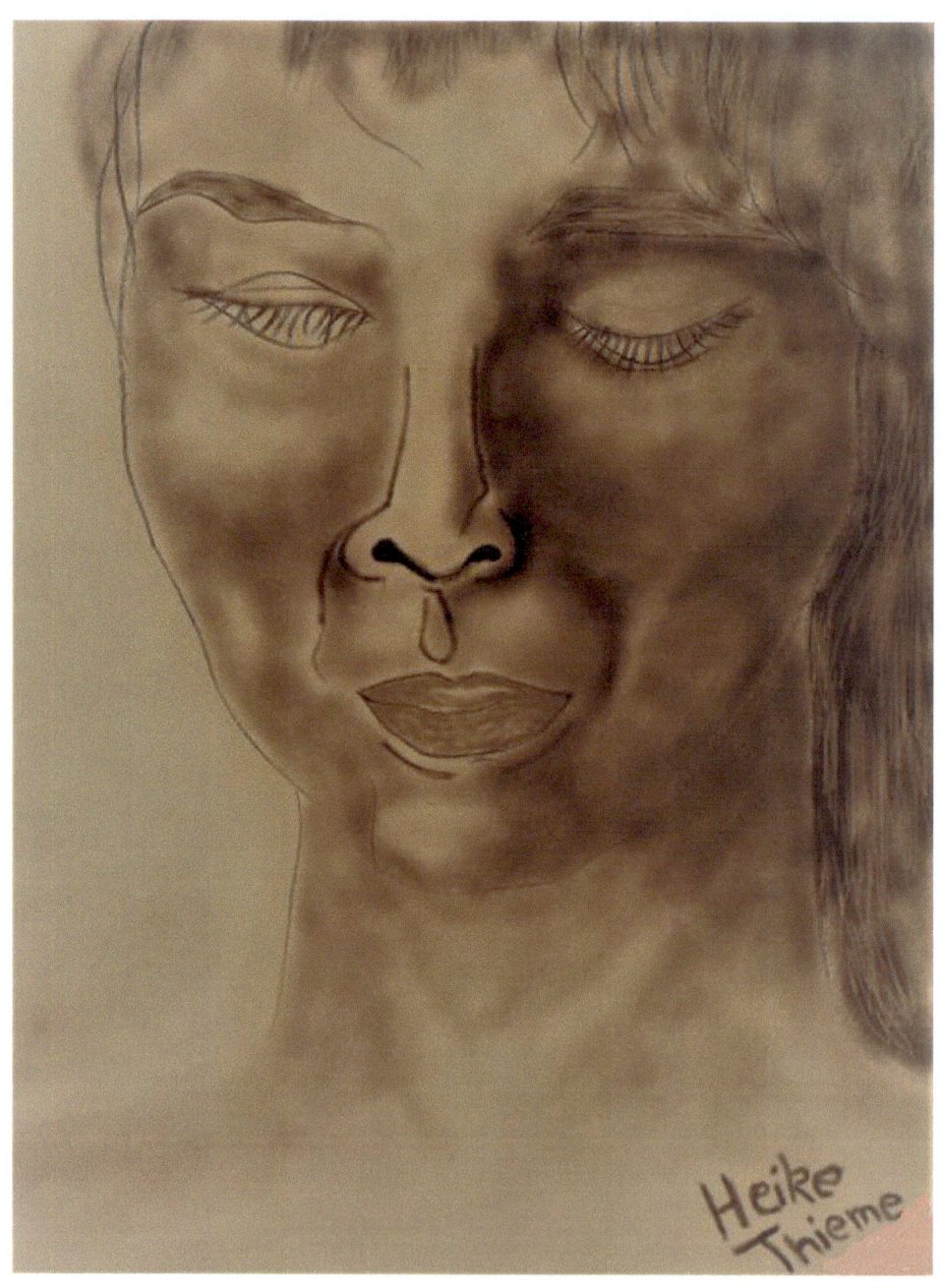

84

Dan Magnus Lundgren painted a fairy figure, a mix of Red-haired woman, lizard, dragon or troll ! I have had a dream again... being among thousand americans, that first time i dreamed that five years ago, thinking being living in a small wooden hutt in my woods, and then on my birthday travelled 1000 american young people from the south up to me to my party, now i dreamed being on a travel between all those places in public where are americans to be found, like one town after another, and i stayed at hotel rooms, with 1000 of people around me again, and i was in the move from one to the next place or universe, was a stressy life, ahhh and you see, that my usual troubles in living was almost those places where i try to live, and so i dreamed being first found by 1000 people in the lonely woods, and then of course being amont the 1000 and on the run from one spot to another, that is my innerst wish to have in my life and living peace !

People in cities are constantly standing and working as if they were underground, which awakens in them the desire, the constant longing, fantasy and yearning for the sunny part of life outside in nature, and being in nature means that you can endure so much noise and stress every day, but react to it in a very balanced and stable way. I look for nature to maintain inner peace and to feel alive without attacks from sick neighbors, it was inevitable that we both met in a world between the two worlds, from that moment on that you hold a young dog baby on your neck and see it slipping into your blood and veins, you change ! Yes, a dog daily, togetherness means relationship, this has nothing to do with love, this is a steady fact, love just comes and goes... ohhh yesss indeed there are many more than in former times, this is funny to see, when i meet outside sick people who know me for more than 25 years in this town.
If they did not have suicided yet and still greet me, they seem to feel always that strong love feeling from far, but i cannot fullfill their wish to be their mom, but if you just would need them for a private act, then this is a hard core work to make them understand that friendship only existed by helping each other, but you will see that they continue hide the real contacts. Because in kinda relationship this is too much for them, every encounter with them scratches hard aside the love experience and that stresses them.

Yes, but sick people cannot describe what they feel, that makes them afraid, this is their tension, this stops only when they hide in their home place, and shut their doors, and those never let anybody in, inside is a mess. A social worker in the children hospital joked with me, i love to provocate the smokers at the huge ash can when i pass and laugh about them, or remind them of the good good breathe, that last one jokes back, he said "We have to smoke, because that is too much cost, if we stop, then they raise the tax immense and we all would go broke !" so i said "Ahh, then it is much better if you all stay sick !" hahahaha

What woman doesn't love the look on her face when she says:
"I can do Kung Fu, I love this sport!" while her husband is already doing something else, just as he is deliberately cheating. Mrs. Lavinia from the Westerwald claims to be the smartest in the Westerwald, which is why she makes a career out of a CV of fraud, and can marry any man she thinks is approachable. Love - a double-edged sword. The Kung Fu thing is far-fetched, while Lavinia is giving her husband a hand.

I have 60 years of successful school and working time to show for it !
Preschool preparation 1 year, Primary school 4 years
High school and all in all 11 school years, Physiotherapy 2 years
Nursing assistant 1/2 year, Voluntary work visiting elderly people 1 year
Secretary assistant 1 1/2 years, Working with the disabled 5 years
Writing 20 years, 118 publications to date, Publishing and reading art,
Single parent 17 years, family abused me, still presents me as an idiot !
I have the right to express my objections ! Teachers don't have an epic.
The dried-up old teacher, of rigid structures,
so unloved that...nobody satisfies her in private,
who hates men so much, that she calls everyone a wimp,
and sees them as fashionably unsuitable,
if the man "stands" in front of her like a so-so,
but in secret she stands there with her arms folded, ready to fight,
believing that one day the chosen one will come, who will take her so hard,
that she will hear the bells ringing !

Official teacher an outsider, a sycophant,
actually a pervert, watched the fist-raising virgin girls
on the leisure spot, in his colorless sandals, just an individualist,
one asks oneself, "What's bothering you?"
"Do you need a piece of chocolate to relieve your stress?"
"Don't you want to let off some steam?"
"We're a closed society!"
"Why don't you have a family?"
"Do you like being the odd one out, without asserting yourself?"
"You'd love to be the center of attention!"
"There seems to be no interest in the chemical formula,
which probably embodies your entire passion, doesn't it?"

The person who officially declares "TEACHER",
who comes to the very last point, so to speak, who wants to lead the way as
a chosen example of the so-called integrity of youth as such,...
my "Dear Mr. Singing Club" who...only differentiates, divides,
subordinates, assesses people in a morally questionable way,
authoritatively excludes, prays, judges, tortures,
praises himself in Latin, builds his rights out of misfortune,
promotes right-wing conservative attitudes, gives his two cents where it is
inappropriate, unfeeling, devalues, incites and agitates,
despite embarrassing sexism towards colleagues,
as a long-forgotten species establishes old customs and order.
It is believed to be the last thing the school thinks about when it comes to
the well-being of its students. TEACHER with their PSYCHO SHIT, real
kind of JUSTICE GAP, where TEACHER sees themselves as important:

A woman becomes a thug, who beats young girls,
because a pretty girl stole the pop star from her in her first love.

An informer becomes a hypocrite, who is after a high position,
because he is made false promises, who ignites a never-ending envy.

A pornographer becomes unsuccessful, who puts science above everything else, because he never shares chemistry with people, a suppressed sexism simmers within him.

An adulterer becomes an unfeeling relationship breaker, who enjoys the fact that people with a bad conscience always go home well during the liaison, and really make a lot of effort in the affair.

A fraudster becomes the opposite of a role model, who collects money that is not his due, while blackmailing those who know about it, ruining their careers if it is revealed, and asking poorer people to pay as a rich bogeyman.

FOR ME THE WORD IS

AN ACTION TO PUT THINGS

IN ORDER,

TO AWAKE THE LOVE IN YOU,

NOT TO SEARCH FOR THE MEANING OF LIFE

BUT TO CONSIDER IT POSSIBLE !
- Heike Thieme - YLVA -
That's how it goes in families! Not everyone lets that happen to them!

Leave your worries and pain behind before they reach you.

It is painful to have a permanent smile on your face and you miss it in your heart. Just respect your heart, it's the only one that thinks you are the best.

If you see them happy with others, don't be fooled because that's how they were with you when they first met you.

Men are also bullies, against their wives,
because they think they are mermaids, who have no legs,
who cannot move, whose only refuge is their imagination,
so they like to be influencers, and the only lapdog for comfort
is the husband's nicknamed Rottweiler,
whose great "empire" is within four walls,
and a marriage that does not change, perhaps the dog already wore the chain
that once adorned the wife's neck, perhaps he thought her after the wedding
was dry, frigid, or a ghost, who could stand without perfume,
what other women smell like.
This is a loneliness in the neighborhood unit, woman in the house,
imprisoned, not studied, not emigrated, not lived out, not swept away,
not shared in love, not refined, not put aside and revived,
not taken on the debts, not played "catch the fisherman",
not played the fish in the house, that was left behind the aquarium without
water, woman also enjoys Hitchcock, the whole neighborhood "just fun",
everything according to the rules,
the woman lived there isolated but inconspicuously.

This is the babble, in Schleswig a welcome greeting for mothers,
which you shouldn't actually say like that:
People, mothers, women don't fall for it. Whoever steals and sits at the table
the smoked fish, the cat has caught it, the mother has the stolen fish with her
kittens at the table and eats what she caught !
Looking at my example, I am in a completely different position
than the parenting clientele, referred to as "The Group",
because I was always so alone, there was only one person for me,
and he didn't even know about me.

I once went into the light,
the sky was blue,
the world so far away,
the earth in the forest,
the game so close,
the mountain was soon there,
I walked along the rock,
with long strides and quickly,
flew into the sun, was gone,
the stars turned to night,
the nightingale sounded,
soon on my feet in the north,
paying no attention to the city.

It has remained that way to this day !
CAPTIVATED, they are EXCITED!
WHAT HAVE YOU DONE TO PEOPLE AGAIN?

Everyone who has grieved knows that.
There are certainly a hundred examples
of people giving their life for the deceased.
One person will definitely get on the wrong bus.
He will hardly find peace alone in the forest.
He will see the dead person fall at his feet.
He would die for love as a clown.
He would take the side of hookers who mourn him.
He wouldn't know whether they should address him as "Sie" or "Du".
He would find his love where it was destroyed.
He would pretend to the world that his heart was in mourning.

It's just right again. During the first WW they envied the lives of kings,
During the second WW they stole the butter from education's bread, -

Now during the third WW they envy children's innocence and attack them!
It didn't matter whether they raped young women, as Russians, as American
soldiers, or perhaps as Turks. They put all these women into almost lifelong
mourning. That's how it is. But it didn't help anyone. Not even the voyeurs
of society! SCARED, they are EXCITED!
WHAT HAVE THEY DONE TO PEOPLE AGAIN?
Who would gain by sitting on a child and taking his breath away,
without thinking, that he would act with such cowardice,
NEVER do the same to an adult? They are only confronted
when the signal is given to actually try to escape!
The quiet feeling is there again in the evening that the perfect married life
is not going to happen, and the "butcher" on the other end,
the recently "wanted" person, or THE RECENTLY "wanted" person,
and ZACK, what turns off a brain?
The evil look says, "Watch out, we have to get out of here!"

The stupid thing since time immemorial, it will follow the word,
because the REWARD is on CHILD FUCKERS !! the female version, that
plays the traditional cannibal. You know the female version?

First one of them sticks out her ass.
Then she keeps a man for herself to have fun with.

First she sacrifices one of the children to the pervert.
Then she offers it up, in a neighborly way no less.

First it's enough for the voyeurs for a while.
Then they want to sacrifice grown women.

First they fight for a career. Then they sense that there won't be one.

First they eat their own grandmother as mincemeat.
Then they need to spoil their victim.

First they love to play "the helper" in their own, clumsy way.

Then they can't watch their victims run away for fear of loss.

First they have fun, then it ends bitterly.
Then their loss has to manifest itself in a bestial way.

Cannibals.....have a death wish, they swear that one day they will make the
world laugh as bad clowns. Every child was born with a laugh, but they
probably had to grunt so loudly while laughing during the first act that they
must have lost the joy of first love ! The active evil seek their consolation in
the other person, full of guilt, and longing, and remorse, and the knowledge
of love and the grief for words not spoken, because they know that they are
giving the last straw the knife into the hand of those who are being hurt,
with the sentence "Just be yourself!" in the false belief that as soon as
someone unloved like that leaves, their evil demon will be defeated !

Being faithful is nonsense. If you are incapable of love,
you demand total loyalty. If you long for closeness so much,
you think that a penis is not for resuscitation, but strange as it sounds,
the thing in the test tube represents "Jesus from Andalusia",
and no improvisation fits. So monogamy is absolute nonsense!

Does the housing association have such a good strategy,
put sick and crazy people in the houses and wait,
with Rolex on their arm and link bracelet, the clock hand on the table,
no computer or email, the little email witch on the shelf with a stick,
the board who knows so they can wait
when the whole new wave of incapacitations starts,
crazy people are causing trouble under every roof,
in their Diakonie apartments, but are allowed to do ANYTHING,
all evidence is dismissed, everything is "a bit too thin" they say,
there was no option either to be evicted again,
a good 9 years, and nobody is giving up! The board is already ashamed,
and still no greetings, as if everyone had a dick on their forehead,
No one, no matter how sick, has laid me low,
that an eviction or incapacitation procedure with the aim of
getting people who speak out openly about it out of the way,
using the means of putting an incited sick person forward
and driving them crazy. BECAUSE BAVARIA WANTS IT THAT WAY,
and they FINALLY want to celebrate in COMMON RETIREMENT
on RÜGEN, to overturn a CITIZEN'S LAW, and to incapacitate people
again at random ! A bit of RUDE-SICKNESS but clever,
an "EXPERIMENT" started about 20 years ago.

The umbrella we use to protect ourselves from the rain in the air is our
parents. If we lose them, rain falls on our heads. The author says.
Ahmim.mourad. I answer - If the umbrella is my parents and my love for
them is the sun, then why did their sun burn me almost as hot as the sun?
Why has the rain come out of my eyes in rivers all my life out of grief?

Who never saved me from anything, but wished me every misfortune and emotionally excluded me from the age of 3, all together?
I also say, "NEVER ATTACK THE SMALL AND WEAK!"
Your word in God's ear....! You don't know where the umbrella is and the umbrella doesn't know you.

I'm sorry, but you don't know the truth. Or maybe I'm hiding the truth from you. Remember these words all your life You don't know where the umbrella is, and the umbrella doesn't know you. In times of pain and sorrow, I pondered over every twin case, and watched every twist in the cold heart of a human being, it is my father who is already standing there before me, as the twin who strangled his twin, and with his arms hanging, why should I thank him for this?

If it is not the truth, I am sure of it, an orphan will see his umbrella by chance... only discover it again in another life! If it is certain that you do not know where the umbrella is and the umbrella does not know you, then perhaps the man is also designed to hide the truth from the woman, and to conceal it from the woman when they meet.

Then I say Solong, and I don't care, they won't make me report this sick girl, not to put myself in danger, and as my good lawyer told me, there would be no other consequences for me, this girl would rise to mainjack, and I would have the total problem, but the housing association may have done nothing about it, nothing more than wait for ME to be the one to leave, as a person who is no longer wanted. The easiest way out for them ... and finally to say "it's summer time!!" the association really knows that I didn't have the slightest chance of legally making the sick person follow the advice of her carers, calm down or leave. This program does the opposite. It silences intelligent and public servant people like me. These landlords play God and are paid by the church. When this sick old chick from above wants to exert power over everyone living below her, she knows she had free reign, so she doesn't have the perception to understand without reason why or how senseless her actions are. She doesn't have reason and doesn't have the basic

communication skills to respond to my frequent statements. You know, any harm done to one will not reflect on them since they gave others "everything"...but this sick way, JUST AN ABUSE OF THE STATE.
She doesn't know how people like her are manipulated by it. So I say solong and don't worry and don't be afraid of what's coming and see her tragic noise as just a normal everyday noise that all people have in a house. And I'm not panicking either because this is going to take a long time and I may continue to blame her for it by making a behavior about it public. And most of all, I'm now celebrating a nice summer with good conversations outside and neighbors who actually like me and Mable, and the sick girl won't be the topic of our conversations. I know the worst way to blame an asshole is always to ignore them.

It's not about denouncing people's marriage with all your might. It's more like two fish walking on two legs! As I said, it's daring for a small child to run up to two children, giving them a malicious look, and the same small child at the same eye level sticks out its tongue with an ice cream stick and a cheeky look back. It's also hard to understand how the ugly thorn hedge is designed to cause serious pain to dogs passing by with the cut thorns on the sidewalks, not expecting that the people around it won't notice and will criticize the dog for being unfriendly. How unavoidable it is when an ugly woman comes rushing up from a distance, deliberately giving all passers-by, near and far, an angry look, but no one takes any notice of her because they are all busy with their children, walking aside, passing by on their bikes, smiling and fresh from school as friends, congratulating each other on having made it today, amigos! Even a stubble haircut would be of no use to a bourgeois who walks across the street towards you with the intention of running you over in a bad mood, but no one has taken any notice of him since the end of time. How could it even be possible then if a fascist feminist got off her bike and turned into the road so aggressively that people would have no choice but to take cover from someone like that because it is well known that women like that kick hard from the back. How can you tell that sympathy in this country is only given to those who have deeply honest feelings for children and express this out of gratitude to the child. After all, who wouldn't admit that they'd be better off minding their own business because no one is going to do it for them?

Greetings are also possible from a distance and are a sensitive gesture of letting the other person be who they are, as long as they don't ask you for help ! No, we are not all the same, we are individually who we are, but the mass is different, more livable and easier to manipulate, that's why I avoid sports fans. The goal of this crap is to destroy trust in politics, to wipe out the free press, to divide the freedom of equality before the law, to displace popular sovereignty, to prevent the masses from demonstrating and free, open speech, to turn the judiciary into a party judiciary that helps the right, or at least to destroy the basic law of a democratic system. They cause nonstop stress to keep people away from real politics. When they stop waiting for real facts and good plans for the future, they say, "Solong, what a load of crap, a more honest person can maybe be true after all." They sneak in through the back door without society ever knowing what's going on until it's over. This happens everywhere, including in Sweden, but with the last war this will end because after this no one will come here to rebuild everything, that is, our human chance was the only one to finally become mature beings, or everything will end VERY quickly.
Don't do things by halves, and people who do things by halves may retire, but you will not live as long as those who told you to live in chaos are not the ones who will help you put the place in order. Don't accept that the psychos become authoritarian against you.

This is all like everywhere else these days that societies seem to be very polarized for the coming elections, and the percentage is about half right and half left, so for all European countries it will be our future hard work not to slide into right-wing doctrines. America now wants publicity in this way, to show the rest of the world how the right-wingers have already taken the Power Tower, to show how quickly a chosen pig will rip the pages of law and order and democracy out of the American manifesto. This will take maybe a few months and then the book of democratic laws in the American way that we knew WILL BE GONE will be blown up.

HERE in Europe it is different, you saw that Poland has now voted the right-wingers off the table, so in England a big rip-off is being ended. The French know what depends on it, as do we all, and the rest of us do not make fun of the French, because this danger lurks everywhere. I SAY these creeps play their games with all societies. They influence the media and cause panic, put people under stress, shock them, spread fake news, fear of the future, hate speech and all that crap. They know which button to push to play and boom, they get more votes because the stressed people just want their peace back and say "Solong" and vote wrong to stop the pressure. They just need a few people in the judiciary and cheat journalism, the right to free speech, free demonstration and so on. Then they have lured society into totalitarianism faster than any normal society would ever experience. A guy like Johnson blamed the English people and panicked them with so much stress that they voted wrong. All it took was a wrong guy.

Imagine this funny picture, when I was in the meadow today with the old apple trees and cherry trees and bee hotels with tall grass and this damn comfortable little thing to lie on, listening to all the birds for an hour in sunshine, between morning rain and evening rain, then I saw this funny picture... a few ugly women came out of one corner after another and all of them were jogging but were not so attractive, as if jogging would make them prettier, and one was a fat little girl in a pink t-shirt jogging step by step, and the mum following behind like a hawk and jogging all around each other... I found it so funny, the ugly ones everywhere and then the older couples, all the women today wearing such African white hats and with them their ancient husbands who had to listen to them, as if the old men were not already blinded enough by life, but their old wives led them home. Life can be funny too, you just have to leave your home. I could imagine that these ugly old and young girls might also have been the OWL's daughters, and she took care of them all.
Money is printed by banks. Material assets are not invisible.
Institutions are puffed up, debts are their own capital. Debts grow.
Citizens work hard, their money - worn out by small money laundering.
Capital income in a triangle, skimmed three times over.

People who bring their money to the bank have fallen for it,
even politics can be financed, by bluffing and the mountain grows,
just because the institutions are largely becoming too expensive,
that the financial world and politics are heading for an abyss !

Nobody will be able to invest 1 cent as long as seed, pesticide and ancillary
costs are rising so much and are subsidized. That is well known.
The farmers must be brought together to form large-scale operations,
which give land to the big companies, there is no other way.
The farmers can only survive if they reach a certain standard,
that is the reality worldwide, and there is also a change in thinking.
If you think big, you sell cheaply, that is the only way to find buyers !

I only decide who I consider an asshole as a friend, and not which assholes
would like to know me in the future! Anyone who acts like an asshole is
educated or ignored. I taught him how to behave. I know that the worst way
to blame an asshole is always to ignore him, do you know how i see the sick
madame ? i see her outside standing now called "Gisela" she is aging, and
recieves retirement for nothing, no work but handicapped privilege, eats
outside that is cheaper, and still thinking "ohh, i am keeping that age of 29"
while once her teetch are lying in her rollator and the titts are hanging
above... do you know why then i won't choose her to be my best A-hole
friend ? because i don't have to !

The Alpha was assigned to the association of those with learning difficulties,
if his home has enough money, at least "money like oil" you eat all the time,
then the caterpillar says "it's beautiful", while he was chairman it was
certainly said that he had distinguished himself militarily, which was later
revealed to be fake, his participation in Vietnam, saving the soldiers, was
simply made up, which George W. Bush admitted, but he was president of
the show and promoted the local cheerleading club. I assume so !

Is the American Dream perhaps a guy who dreams to be Callboy ?
Is it well known, they have fable for Asian, Vietnamese Women,
where they call them Lovers of US-veteran,
or is it the holy day of the Male Fairy, used to find over as Fairy Princes ?
Is the American a passionate fan of Circus Arena and Roman fighting ?
Is that kinda maybe a friend of the octopodes ?
Is the American style of man to cuddle until the doctor is coming ?

In the same way, the question does not arise as to whether the creature that
was found in Scotland was a prehistoric monster. The real monster, if you
ask the woman at the gynecologist, is the gynecological chair. The woman
concluded that such a chair was found on the shore of the lake and that it
was radioactive, because the monster for the hole was therefore named
Loch Ness.

There are also regions in our country
where people are not so interested in letters,
which is why there is no need for a post office, or a carrier pigeon,
or a delivery person who struggles to move his bike everywhere.
They are illiterate people who can communicate quite well without
that is, in other words. They make music. The transmission of thoughts is
also very special in it, it doesn't cost a penny and it helps.

If you are exposed to humiliation, look for the son of the lion, he is the only
one who stands by your side.
says the philosopher Ahmim.mourad

I know that son is my son. He is one of those sons of the lion.
He is my only family and protective. He is a womanizer as i know him.
- Heike Thieme - Ylva -

Before today I hadn't thought about what life is like without an address?
Sharing mail at collection points. Nothing more. It's incredibly peaceful -
the thought of being completely free of bureaucracy and official fuss!

Being watched by birds
is not as frightening as feeling
the liberation of being replaced by other people's families...
I don't even fear being in the wet,
fragrant grass, being plagued by fat snails,
and not being able to lie there in the winter.

Do you know how i see the sick madame ? i see her outside standing now
called "Gisela" she is aging, and recieves retirement for nothing, no work
but handicapped privilege, eats outside that is cheaper, and still thinking
"ohh, i am keeping that age of 29" while once her teetch are lying in her
rollator and the titts are hanging above... do you know why then i won't
choose her to be my best A-hole friend ? because i don't have to !

I think she might have a strong loss or reality perception, but enough of it
trying to humiliate me since so long. I think she might have a strong loss or
reality perception, but enough of it trying to humiliate me since so long.
She is depend on so much, like medicine, doctors, therapy and eating
outside, that she might even have a big tick in mind, but that made her
depending on so many, that she meant to give her life stress on my back.
I think her biggest trouble she went through the most was her midlife crisis
phase now, wait i had a thought about that chick today.

I also say: "NEVER ATTACK THE SMALL AND WEAK!" Your word in
God's ear...! You do not know where the umbrella is, and the umbrella does
not know you. I am sorry, but you do not know the truth. Or maybe I am
hiding the truth from you. Remember these words all your life. Maybe the
man is also destined to hide the truth from the woman and to conceal it from
the woman when they meet. But as innocently small as she appears in her
trousers and high heels and her boyish cap, she is actually estimated to be
about fifty years old, or is already approaching sixty, so she is definitely not
as young as she thinks. She never says hello, is tense, shies away from the
neighborhood. The rural innocence she pretends to be is a ridiculous
grimace under pure show.

I only decide who I meet as an asshole as a friend, and not which assholes would like to know me in the future! Who is an asshole plays, is educated or is ignored. I taught him how to behave. I know that the worst way to blame an asshole is always to ignore him, you know how I see the sick madam? I see her standing outside now, her new name is "Gisela", she's getting old, getting a free pension, has no job but a disability allowance, eats outside which is cheaper, and still thinks "ohh, I'm keeping my age of 29" with her teeth in her walker and her tits hanging over it... do you know why I won't choose her as my best asshole friend then? Because I don't have to!

In times of pain and grief, I have thought about every twin case and watched every twist in the cold heart of a person. It is my father who is already standing in front of me, as the twin who strangled his twin, and with his arms dangling. Why should I thank him for this? Two fish would rather walk on two legs! If it is not true, which I am convinced is true, an orphan will see his umbrella in passing... and only rediscover it in another life! Then I say Solong, and I don't care, they will not force me to report this sick girl so I don't put myself in danger, and as my good lawyer told me, there would be no further consequences for me, this girl would push herself to the forefront and I would have the total problem, but the housing association may have done nothing about it, done nothing more than wait for ME to be the one to leave, as a person who is no longer wanted.

Easiest way out for them... and to say "It's summer time!!" Society really knows I didn't have the slightest chance of legally getting the sick woman to follow her caregivers' advice to calm down or leave. This program does the opposite. It silences intelligent and public service people like me. These landlords are playing God and getting paid by the church. When this sick old chick from above wants to exert power over everyone living under her, she knows she had free reign, so she doesn't have the perception to understand without reason why or how senseless her actions are. She doesn't have reason and doesn't have the basic communication skills to respond to my frequent comments. You know, any harm done to someone will not reflect on them since they gave "everything" to others... but in this sick way.

SHE IS SIMPLY AN ABUSE OF THE STATE. She doesn't know how people like her are manipulated by it. So I say keep going and don't worry and don't be afraid of what's coming and consider her tragic noise a perfectly normal everyday noise that all people have in a house. And I don't panic either because this will take a long time and I may continue to blame her for it by making a behavior about it public. And most of all I'm now celebrating a nice summer with good conversations outside and neighbors who really like me and Mable and the sick girl will not be the subject of our conversations.I know the worst way to blame an asshole is always to ignore.

But I understand that you have laughed with me many times and cried alone too. This one woman who lives above me is an aging mentally ill person, no matter what her problem is, I don't care. No one wanted to have to share the neighborhood with someone like that, under any circumstances. What I recognize is that she lives in therapeutic contact with assisted living facilities and eats out, never worked. The facility rented her the apartment so she is untouchable and unassailable and with that knowledge she knows that she was allowed to take her anger out on me almost every day and night for nine years in an uninterrupted and humiliating way without any evidence. There is no getting to her. She dresses like she is twenty-one, carries a backpack like her little school bag, carries bags full of candy, crafts, balloons and gifts from her daycare home and pushes everything home in a rolling suitcase.

You see a woman there on the street, when she stands up straight her face has grown old. She is really holding on to this memory of being very young and age shows the opposite, no I know these people from work and they have no idea what their moods, emotions and changes are, they react from one point to another without any reason. They chose me as a buffer zone so the girl can train her emotional outcast and call that her way of healing. The weird girl belongs in the soup, but her age has made it better. She has to accept that she is no longer a pretty young girl. No, so I say, such an old girl does not belong in my soup.

But you only get your feelings back when you are far away.

There was the little ring I found in the sand, the pearls shimmered a little blue. And also again an Yggdrasil ring, for the second time in the same place, these are rings that belong to me if I don't take the ring off once. One of the little wolf rings in the ring once had a sharp point and it hurt when I took it off, and I have another ring in my drawer, only made of silver, and it had my son's date of birth and name on it, a silver ring makes my eyes relax. So people see that this woman is also pretending to have a great golden future in a transmigration of souls when she repeatedly manages to drive the people living below her out of the house, openly pretending to be a psychopath, whether in female or male form, they compulsively act the same. Both are chosen by God, but neither senses that they are going up and back to hell. Real friends are simply too smart to behave like bad people! This is how you can tell them apart from normal people. In my opinion and experience with psychopaths, it is easy to see that in this clientele they are in fact real bunglers. Their big dream was over.

When I openly explained to her one morning in the middle of our hallway in the presence of one of her carers, as a neutral stranger, how this person had been humiliating me and making noise for so many years, making my life difficult, even though I had no option to leave here, and I expressed to her several times that I did not want to do anything to her or harm her, with the announcement of consequences if she wanted to understand this correctly. This is the danger for all people, whether man or woman, if they come into contact with a shiny, bright and big heart, they are all made fools of. And from today on I will leave her lying in the gutter like a wet rag, everyone can smell from afar where the sheep are going. Predators. She should let them tear her to pieces. I have nothing to do with this person! It is paradoxical when people know that the privilege of life that was given to them because they were not abused, if they were lucky enough to not be on the same side as the victims. On the other hand, this disabled woman is not in control of her awareness of reality, at least her perception is very different from the normal world. I know many who know that they do not know the whole truth about everything and do not want to know it.

104

You see, that is human! But in her case, she is trying to turn the tables, to
make my life difficult because she is dependent on care and is probably very
unhappy with her life because she is not self-determined.
But I still do not care. Go to Wallachia.
You don't give a damn about the city.
You go over to the Silent Land. Past the king's castle.
You stand on the wall, in your robe.
You wanted to avoid catching what was coming from above.
You waved his flag around your ears. You let one go, he had flown away.
Don't you see the lithe women. They went to pick up dung in just rags.
What a king who wore glasses. And those who wore glasses
were punched in the mouth, they called it "Shut up!" by the mob!

SEX horror, but there are no sources that show
that forced chastity with a pussy belt existed,
the whole thing was almost impossible, but in the opposite sense
it was possible that when the man was absent,
the professional dildo offered the most times they were all alone
its services to women !

The most frequently spoken sentence
about the idolized brother,
about the son hated by the mother,
about the writer hated by the sister,
about always being put on a pedestal by the partner,
about the longing for peace and quiet,
about the grief for the deceased son,
about the worry for the parents - such driven, trivial nonsense
leads him over and over again to talk
about how he is the eternally unloved one, and his sister is broken by it,
as an idealist, trembling with anger and do-gooderism,
her feelings of guilt drive her to fits of tears,
but finally both take themselves far too seriously,
without taking any notice of the other.

People respect those who have money, but honesty and frankness are appreciated by only a few.

when Sister envies
my willing to survive,
she is no better than killing me,

when Brother envies
my ability to laugh at men,
they were carelessly and grey brothers.

There is a big difference, a very VERY big one, because you have not experienced everything I have in your entire life. According to my CV, I am unfortunately not capable of being in a relationship. I am sorry about that, other people say the same. We are not getting any younger, unfortunately. I say to talented friends, you have certainly traveled far and wide on your own, thanks to your sound language skills! What I am saying is that I don't want to start a relationship with anyone, actually with no one at all, and certainly not with younger men. I don't have a girlfriend or a close friend who can always see me sitting alone, but I lived this life to be alone, if only to survive this family that I had inside me, and that works fine, but not in terms of lasting closeness to one person. If I had been looking for closeness, I would have studied at a university; I study everything and the world in my head. I am one of those street kids too; they don't commit to anything. But it is good for me because someone can philosophize with me. What I mean by that is, no, I'm sorry, don't come to me, you have to look for someone else in this country, I can't handle a man in this life. You are a lion, my son is like you, and this acquaintance would burn me like a piece of paper, if you don't accept that, our conversation must end here. My door as a friend is open to you.

You won't believe it, but this place managed to heal me and my dear dog protected me. There is no wrong place in this world, there is only you, who doesn't defend yourself. I didn't get sick there, or sicker, but I became a strong fighter. I have a chameleon-like neighbor. As trivial as it sounds, I mean my apartment neighbor. She has been subtly oppressing me for nine years because she is very ill. You would think it's because she hears me talking to my dog, because I have to laugh out loud, and because I live as a free person. I know how important it is to travel. But I didn't have the money for that. I tried everything to defend myself against this person, but she uses her illness privilege to be untouchable.

The fact that I have said all this very honestly is also an attempt to face the facts, and since I am not a blank slate or a simpleton, a speechless blank slate, and have learned my limits, I now also recognize better where other people's limits are and try not to hurt anyone with the help of my honesty. Being clear and honest is the only thing that helps in life. It is not just a matter of surviving on the whole. It is also the case that I recognize that I am not a hero. I am glad that there are real friends. But as long as we do not merge into one another like two birds of paradise, we cannot beat each other's heads in or end up hating each other.

Russia will collapse if Trump does not gain a majority in America. Yes, let us all hope so! I cannot imagine how a large, democratic country like the USA could sink so low as to put a misogynistic, anti-democratic criminal like him on its golden throne; then their country would sink into chaos. Anyone who lives in Israel is full of fear; oh dear, poor Israel and everything there and around it, all the beautiful places that I visited, are gone. Even when I was at school, it was more important to me to form my own opinion of history and to definitely travel to Israel at some point and confront it, so I dropped out of school and, whoosh, six months later, I was there too. Dropping out of school was the trigger; I was brutally disowned by my family. Fighting is nature's invitation, Whoever accepts will make progress. The world has changed. People are starting to think like machines. We drink water that tastes bad.

Israel.

Yes, it was definitely a beautiful country. First I saw the beach. Sometimes you see beautiful flowers growing in a bad place. We ask ourselves how? haha, all I know is that sleeping where rats can survive means never losing your sense of humor again, all I'm saying is that where there is enough water, any flower can make it, and a woman can bloom anywhere!

Flowers grow even in France, where at least 100 nuclear power stations are radiating. There are spiteful people everywhere, oh, I don't know, Africa is more of a country of business. Only in Europe is it so deeply embedded in thinking that they secretly make fun of it and yet still benefit from the cleverness of others.

Yes, I think women from everywhere have the resource or substance to make this world a more beautiful place because they think about environmental politics. No, I just believed in how I managed to make an upright person out of my only son all by myself. And I'm not in a church. The day could come one day when there could be more peace, then the different religions would realize that it can only work together. That's what I'm waiting for. For me, cultural sites are interesting buildings. However, I think that for children or people who live out on the street, survival is not dependent on a pretty, well-carved 2000-year-old building, but on learning the BASICS of how best to avoid danger.

I imagine it, like an owl in a dressing gown,
like a sausage in a dressing gown,
like a sausage in a pastry shell, like börek,
like three steps to the left, and three steps to the right,
and getting married, dying, everything starting again from the beginning!
If you call politics today, you think of how radically
right-wing they want to be, like Roman games,
including slapstick theater on stage,
open-air concerts and disabled players
who are put on display, there is no need for talent anymore,
because whoever denies the truth, also admits that he can't do anything !

The Middle Ages blamed everything,
even the cold winters, on women.
The industrial age ruined everything
in terms of illness, pollution, contamination,
even the possible future of one's own children
for profit, including the children.
Instagram left everything,
even the ridiculousness of the portrayal,
to the stupidest people to become known.
Today's world advocates for the future,
and does greenwashing drives petrol cars,
egoists at top speed on the highway. ...
so much for the general political situation,
the epidemics, and the threat of poverty,
there is hardly any time stopping the wars,
to do anything about the climatic situation !

You are something like a brother to me, the kind I always wanted.
But also a Nostradamus who tells the world all the downfalls our world is
facing! Sorry, but I don't think of you as Mr. Doomsday!

That wasn't what I meant, I hope you can forgive me! Do I want to know
what will happen to you or the flower? No, I find predictions like that scary.
If I were to compare myself to the flower, if I had all the problems of rainy
summers, cold winters, years with little growth, years that bear no fruit,
poor nutrition, too much fertilizer, etc. then I would rather remain human,
because I don't even need an umbrella, because I love the rainwater on my
skin, I just wish for you, my brother, that you grow well and thrive.
No, I don't believe that either, a flower would be the last of all to die. It is a
child of Mother Heaven and Earth, who does not abandon her children.

The flower has never asked when it will open its blossom, it simply knows
that it will. The flower does not need fruit to bloom, and it is so cheerful that
it is certain that if the year is wet, the sun will shine next year.

Yes, if the earth died, we would not live to see it, but before that it can swell up into a ball of fire and leave us in a huge torrent of illuminating fireworks, and only then will there be peace, what kind of insect are people that wants to decide whether the good old earth finds peace or not? A lot of worry these days, but who brings me to a church to worship the poor starving body on the cross as a mere fictional character, so that I can carry all its suffering, like that of all the others, on my shoulders and hopefully enter heaven with grace? If only one walk through the meadow, the swamp or under the trees makes me so happy in just one hour that I can find my way home, relieved of everything? If you have spent just one time as a young girl on an island in absolute peace, I will never forget that absolute moment. At first I was surprised at my family, who always stayed in the house and never understood why I always had to be outside, but then I saw clearly that these people could not even see me as a human being, so in their delusion I had become indifferent to them. Only people who have grown up in the way people once inhabited the earth are knowledgeable, and it is precisely such people who will always be our teachers, because they see everything about us, feel it when we recognize, research, learn, and praise us. They feel happiness as if their hearts were flying away with them along with the ladybird. They experience love with every fibre of their being, spontaneously, intensely and lastingly. I believe the knowledgeable are women. They live in an African cave. They are the council of wise women. They know the secret of flying. If you feel it, you don't have to want it, because one day you too will fly. I even believe that men learned to fly before women. Because women are two-pronged, just as firmly rooted in the earth, and they have to put one and one together first. You can travel without leaving your place, but with your mind, the mind is the saddle in which we humans sit. A single ride in such a saddle from one end of the long beach to the other and you have been around the whole world, so I take care not to fall in love. I recognize my dream horse, as it eked out its existence behind bars, and wanted to go with me because we had promised each other, but then I sat alone on the distant beach and cried afterwards because I didn't have it as my horse, from then on I dreamed of searching this world for my horse, orange in its coat, thoroughbred in its heart, kindness in its eyes.

I can't answer that question for you...who is a real woman and who isn't? When I let all my horses go, I had to start out alone, far away, then write all my novels, only then did all the horses fly over me, into their freedom and I belonged to them, so it was no problem for me to finally learn to fly, and it was a woman again, at night in the middle of the unknown city, who showed me the direction of my path. I was thus a nightingale in the starry sky, flying over cities and escaping. I know that sixty years of being alone has told me so much about myself that I know that I will not have a partner in this one human life. I couldn't have done it at seventeen either. I would say the same thing at 127.

Good, then I am a butterfly that nests in the garden that the farmer neglected because he is stupid.

That was only one travel to Israel, very spontaneously. I was in Crete in Greece, and those guys i was travelling in their bus with me, they were kinda boring to me, that i decided to continue by boat to Israel in 3 days, just to have been there once in life, like my schoolmate and i once wanted to. You know those guys were witnessing that my family abondoned me, and i had nothing to bite, and no place to hide, but they were students, lazy people, one lived in a valley, and so he let me live in my indian tent on his garden, but he never ever decided together with me how things may become better for me, and i was too proud to beg for his food, so i got used to never eat for weeks long, no problem, then they invited me to go on a holiday trip to Greece, and i went on a student trip with them, but they were boring people never speak, and had enoug money spending good times, i had nothing, sothen i left that bus finally.

When being back in my tent in that valley they still kept on being ignorant people, even that first days back in Germany an american Soldier had raped me. Nobody cared. That was the opinion of my lawyer i met once who gave me that sharp wording advice to flee as fast as i can, as far as i get to start my new life anew and did never ever come back to my fathers place, who tried to incapacitate me, just in short words said.

Jobs that i learned were physiotherapist, elderly care, work with handicapped and asit in the entrance of a socialworkers office, where to help people with problems to get a work or anything to practice on the market, that was from above church, sothey got to know me as person with knowlegde how to treat handicapped, and i was right away giving many advices, but they never gave me a real working contract even not after six years, sothen they sended me home, so since ten years at last i am unemployed, and live from the state with a kinda half retirement but not so much money. I had to do so many works in life without good payment, so that my retire now is not higher than social money. But finally my father told me to give me a little monthly aside of that. I have never gotten the drivinglicense, and not reached university studies, and my spine causes meanwhile backpain when doing hard works, like in a hotel kitchen i did, and cleaning jobs even the same, my back canno more bear that. I was not keen in my future ? and as well in my home town 45 years ago, i was not only once being raped by men, these were three rapes, none in family who gave me shelter and protection. That is why i am little traumatized, but nowadays am over the past. Not keen on my future, was not easy for me, to bear a hard trauma, to change the towns, to never drive a car, not get good paid jobs, indeed, but then raise one child alone, and you still get no good jobs, because then the offices say what to be allowed or not, and that is working without salary, until the child is grown, or i might have nothing to feed my son. With that family i had, the problems had started. I would not have chosen such a path myself. But father was afraid that i would once start in the own life and tell the people how they mistreated me at home, so he tried to better kill me with denounce and stalk and spy my life as long as he gets me behind bars, where he could see me die with, better than that i told the people what was happening in my life. So really there is no family behind me, never really was, but those last ten years i wrote and published my experience, life ideas, path, learnings by life and painted good Art, that strengthed me back to my whole being, and so it is those old people and family rests now existing who are pretty ashamed, never had trusted in me. Complete with university or studies ? not possible, after such a rapist trauma, you are almost not able to join in school classes, with bully, with

112

elitary idiots, with racist, with a-holes that i tried so often in life, but one single day you decide that is was enough, those people won't hurt me or others anymore, that i may really good concentrate on conversation, and own ideas, but not learn to read and remember the learning stoff in studies easy, it does not work, and i have one funny problem, that i am not able to work in business offices, with numbers and plans, and mathematic logic things, because often my brain blocks when thinking in numbers, the secretary must know how to think perfect in numbers, check it and Bookkeeping is error-free, companies demand it.

And it was like my father shouted at me, that if i told anything about familiar abuse, he destroyed me with his influence, money and willing. That guy was just locksmith in the military, and was to find out everything i did, he wanted to bring me down make me incapacitated. My lawyer was good enough telling the laws have changed, that a family has not those rights easy anymore to lock me up for just send me spies, because noe I was gone. But later being pregnant my father again spoke to all, and my child was taken away from birth, that i fought 1 1/2 years to get my lovely son back ! That was the last brick of devlish deed of my father.
Once who hurt you that way, he will recieve no single chance anymore !
My son, now is 27, he said clearly, that he needed not that money from family, they won't bring us both apart, even they tried, to get control on his life too. He does not want anything have to do with them, that was the long side of the story.

Is it true, that relationship is just THAT ILLUSION ? as lesser that i experienced my PEACE the lesser people act to be in relation to me, so i don't want the PEACE anymore, and wait for nobody to open me like a can beer, ant left me empty anymore. I am tired, and now or soon go to sleep, when the chameleon will be blessing the house peace.

You see, my friend, in all that long story was never the chance to live a usual partnership life with anybody. That is why i love more that imagination of a Good Friend and Bro, good my father did not stick in me, the few greenhorns who did it, never mind, meant okay wait until those nightmares end, then flee, i did. Then those flashbacks reappeared, and i was quit. I see it, all this repeats in every single street, some too young end with drugs, some like me end in loneliness, but if i did study medicine with that father, and ended with the top of a job, he still tortured my mind. Some say to be poor but live true is far healthier. As much as i wanted my life in peace the more that i fled to relationship, that is soo damn stupid but seems to be a triggering technic of mind, like you said it, the more a woman may imagine to be against all Art, she appears the total acceptance. Is it true, that relationship is just THAT ILLUSION ? as lesser that i experienced my PEACE the lesser people act to be in relation to me, so i don't want the PEACE anymore, and wait for nobody to open me like a can beer, ant left me empty anymore. I am tired, and now or soon go to sleep, when the chameleon will be blessing the house peace.

I know, I know the plans of American soldiers who know exactly that they can do whatever they want. Similar to the Russian cyborgs. They are always people who rape any young woman because... that's exactly how I remember it, my father sent them after me, the first one "served" me so diligently that I wanted to vomit because of his ugliness, the second one "horrified" and "shocked" me because he went to school with me, the third one tried to "break" me, to whom I clearly told him that he would rather kill me, but I would not obey him. It was only exactly after I had completed vocational training at around 25 that I had the first flashbacks - every night for half a year I had the same nightmare that woke me up, I couldn't breathe and thought I was losing all my teeth, at exactly 3 a.m. It wasn't an illusion, it was a dance with the devil, I call him my father.

It was only when I started writing that the flashbacks came back. Half a year later, I almost lost my balance on the way to the post office with my book manuscript in the northern city because my head was spinning violently, but I stood firm. It finally stopped after the 4th book.

It was only after I had published 100 books that the flashbacks came back again. I chatted with the wrong person who sparked a series of nightmares in me, showing me what was behind the whole situation of a young woman being homeless. It was disgusting, but I understood the trigger from then on.

It is only today, with 118 books, that I understand that it was good for me not to have studied, not to be a famous celebrity, not to have become rich, not to have moved from hotel to hotel, not to have many friends, and that rapists started in my parents' house and everything that came after that will eventually be "history" for me.

Real women don't care about that.
Everyone knows that guys compliment them,
and if you do that, you're doing yourself good.
Because most women realize as they get older,
"She always thought that men were interested in women's inner qualities, ... but they only pay attention to what they see!"
a valuable sentence, hahaha, "I thought you looked older!"
I wasn't prepared for so much pity, hahaha.

I once had a conversation with a Russian woman who loved wolves. She had a boyfriend and his friends in Italy, and when she was coldly dumped and felt ashamed and laughed at, her humane attitude and her whole natural philosophy of equal people suddenly changed. She cursed all of Italy and wished death on everyone, just as the serious epidemic broke out at that very time and 50,000 Italians died very quickly.

I immediately broke off contact with her, saying that no one had the right to make such statements just because of a broken love, to wish death on an entire country, and she was blocked... so much for the subject of Russians and love. Unfortunately, I have to say that when it comes to Russian people, I slowly began to suspect that no one should trust them, as they are currently turning into a different kind of person, more like killing machines, cyborgs. They still allow you to speak to them openly, but now there is a sense of threat in the way you look at them. If you have the opportunity to defeat your enemy, you have no pity for him. All of Russia is for sale. Well, and if you tell someone like that, almost directly, the violence he feels, which makes him great, as an educated son of the elite, that you just don't take the young man and pants-shitter seriously for his fantasies of omnipotence because not everyone will throw themselves on the mat for him, then he finds out WHO he is dealing with and you are fundamentally prepared for this conversation and why, then these elite sons become very small and you can smell the shit in their pants! If someone scares me, they will have to deal with ME too!

People who love money are bad.

That's why I haven't seen a male German doctor for twenty years.
They lie to everyone. In future I will only call them by their first names anyway. and a sick woman who had been abused at home just explained to me that her doctor had worried her by telling her that her "cerebellum was shrinking", what a disgraceful, incompetent piece of rubbish! I told her that I was not entirely convinced that she had such an "illness".

It is true that cruel people do indeed do very bad things, but everyone does it within the limits of what is possible, because not everything is allowed in order to keep things from getting boring! Find out where the ghost train is going. Wise people who observe it are actually right, it is the poor population of those who are not given medical help but are made to look so ridiculous.

The girls today, as their physical development shows, are all sexualized at the age of 10, paraded around in front of the neighbors, seduced together, so to speak, then at 15 they are made drunk in front of the eyes of the world to the spectacle of lightning in the black sky at midnight, so that they fall into bed behind their chamber like a sack, and at 17 they already look like a fattened chicken, and are a laughing stock, and feel proud of it. Poor Germany! But they don't notice. I have gone my own way, and that's why I know it. No, I just expressed it in such a way that I refuse to have to save or heal other people who are in need and in emotional distress. I waited long enough for someone to come along who wanted to be healed by me, but no one came. So I decided that if anyone was going to be helped, it would only be myself. I am not a trained doctor, but I am not a person with a helper complex either. No, and no one in this long life has had power over my decisions! I am not a god, that's right. The most that would happen is that a person would like to get drunk with his own kind, then think he is a god, but wake up as a pig.

We remain a mystery in this life.
We are the ones whose features show nothing but calm.
We are the ones who do not turn to anyone when we feel sad.
We heal ourselves no matter how painful we are.
We are the ones who do not surrender to the bitterness of the days, we accept everything that happens silently, then we continue on our path in peace. And peace for our souls when peace is absent from our lives
The days were the same, the people were the same, so we no longer cared about who stayed and who left. The faces around us, the relationships, the feelings, even the pains, shocks, and disappointments were similar. They no longer moved inside us, i.e., but we began to expect them at any time and from any person, no matter how high his position in our hearts. Our feelings were similar, so laughter took the place of crying. We began to laugh at the intensity of our misery and cry when joy overtook us, lost in the midst of similarities, we did not recognize all of them, we were not attracted to any of them, nor were we repulsed either. It has obliterated every pleasure, taken away every pleasure, killed every desire, and frustrated every attempt.

How many people we lost in our lives because we were too real, honest in all the things we offered..We lost because we were unable to fake our feelings and beautify the way we dealt with them. We were unable to be fake and friendly. We were clear and frank. We do not know how to pretend and appear in more than one way. We do not know how to twist and turn or assume a character that contradicts our personality. We do not know hypocrisy, courtesy, and opposition to our convictions and principles. We lost because we did not offer anything except from our depths, because we only care about being ourselves. We lost a lot, but we gained ourselves, and this is the most important gain in our lives.

There is a point that a person reaches. We can call it a point of balance and moderation in feelings. Giving the sacrifice. And looking at life in general. Where things do not affect him as before, perhaps because he finally realizes that neither people nor things are constant. Rather, they change and change with time, and this brings peace and reassurance. Therefore, be selective, as selection is an art, and choose carefully what deserves to be within the framework of your life, and beware of wasting yourself and your time in places, relationships or interests that are not yours, do not resemble you, and do not express you.

A morning message to your heart..
Be optimistic, you deserve life..
Always believe that something wonderful is about to happen.
If yesterday made you sad, what is the fault of today that makes you sad?
Smile, you deserve life. A beautiful day brings new opportunities. Put your worries aside and find a reason to smile. Treat your soul with forgetfulness and fill your heart with love, you deserve to live life and enjoy every moment of it. And in the midst of the pain, smile, let the pain realize that it did nothing significant in your resolve, just water your soul with optimism, and give peace to that beautiful heart that you carry within the sides of your chest. Smile, you deserve the beauty of life. In order to achieve psychological peace, you must do the following:

Trust: Delegate your affairs to the one who holds the keys to the unseen. What God writes for you is good.

Optimism: The future is more beautiful, God willing..
Submission: God destined and did what He wanted, and the best is what God chose.

God will relieve her as if she had never been distressed by us, for our entire life belongs to God. Thanks these are wonderful long wordings.
Very positive. Not authoritive. Very much spoken by heart.

And say, O distant stranger, how do you know distance when you are in your ruin? Did you not see the morning sun or did the stars and the moon block you from life? Oh, winter is snowing. Are you the one who experiences winter on its streets or do you watch it from the train window?

That is it ! The more you live in your heart, and love. The better is distance to be seen. The only one who knows is the one with his wings.

Taking the time to find answers with real questions,
what's stopping you from doing that?
... but it's going to rain in two minutes!
Wriggling around the fact that people on Earth live longer,
what's stopping you from accepting that?
Trying to explain the world to children,
which also shows that they had known it for a long time?
Thanking the one who wears the rose on his lapel,
what could be nicer than ignoring that?

We have spoken outside, the two brothers, sons from a single parent father and me and Mable, we just spoke about of our theory what was first, the egg or the chicken, then i told them shortsaid my version, and the both had many things to complain, was funny, at least we closed that all in the world wether they are muslim, christian or viking, nature believers or even living in an african cave, and on island they all do believe in the right way they want to, and all things to believe in a better future for their region they live in, and none is better than another not the region nor the people with their believe, one friend's wonderful saying and wording from the Koran made me happy very much. Those both kids, brothers are the kids of the single parent father. It feels good having that understanding between, not many think it over, so that everyone may speak and talk with everyone.

Yes, but what would someone say who only runs in a hurry and for money alone catches the early day like the worm and then hides his deepest, strangest personal problems and runs from one place in the world to another, did he miss like the sun and the moon what concerned him? Did the stars think of him, and did he ever understand the real distance in reality? I mean, that is simply the ability to love oneself and think from the heart, then the understanding of distance is understood, not the seeker of inner peace who by force constantly seeks and looks in another place and never finds himself. Then you saw how he knew the snowy winter better and could live with it from the street, or did he simply notice, "Oh, it is winter when I look from the inside of a train at the snow from my window frame!"
One day, I was walking on a street, and suddenly a storm and strong winds came, preventing me from walking. I found a tree on the side of my street and sat under it. Then I raised my head to a tree and saw a dove on a tree branch, shivering from the cold, with sad eyes. I said to her: Why are you sad?   She told me that I was flying in the air with my son until a strong wind blew and I was fighting the wind. I did not notice my son until after the storm had calmed down, and I looked to my side and behind me and did not find my son. Maybe the storm caught him. While she was speaking, tears were falling from her eyes. I said to her: His son is smarter than his mother. She said: What are you saying? I told her: They took the path of the storm, and you walked against the storm. He was on the other street, on top of a pink tree with beautiful flowers. If he had followed your path, he would have been destroyed by the storm, because he is small and cannot resist the wind. That's why he chose to walk downwind.

Der Geist dieser Zeit hält sich
für ... klug,
wie jeder solche Geist dieser Zeit.
Aber Weisheit ist einfältig,
nicht einfach.
Ist es besser, Fragen zu stellen,
die die Zusammenarbeit unterstützen,
oder Fragen, die polarisieren?

I am not famous, but you said it, to write against a storm meant to walk with him, as you see it's true, the novel must be really a novel, so to reach a publisher who brings books in the stores on land.

I see that one good friends style of writing is strong held to real emmigrant, immigrant and travelling the countries, to show how real life may be, with love, familiar bonds, and future planning.

I do hold my thought connected to deeper issue, the heart and mind thing, and the pains and growths. When you write a novel, you must make the reader swim in it like the sea, and then the waves come to him so that he can enjoy his swimming. At the end of the novel, the sun sets on a beach. Through writing, we can control people's minds and we can change their minds. As for the reality that you and Al-Maanat are talking about. People want something that makes them happy, not miserable, perhaps to open a wound again after it has healed.

But as well as the reality meant sameway to me, those talks in most months of the year are the only ones, too, this is a pretty game of conversations and loneliness, but we live here in a strange place of province and town, here connects germany with the nordic, and the tourism from the south, then sea to the left and sea to the right, just a small place in between, so here spoken about five dialects and languages, and all people from far suddenly feel homy here, with much tradition and associations of elderly and people who love to feast and drink among each other, and make their music, or sing in the club. But i was trying but won't belong to people who have money or feast and can't get used to alcohol. These clubs all have their rules, and the outsider and artist like me, would never belong to, not allowed when not been traditional grown up with them and not being the rich class, with house, car, family and job. They like to play so easy come and go, but it is just facade, i would just live here and tell them that i know that town now for real 35 years, and they said "Ask me again when you are living here 65 years, maybe then !" but it is not a big place here, so this is harmless, that i am aware the people that i got to know even 25 years ago and after 25 years seen once again i still know them and know their name. They do the same to me, standing right in front of me, telling me "Haven't i seen you in cinema as visitor once twenty years ago ?"- i tell you this is a kinda strange place here ! I had a grandfather who definitely mostly painted all those Vincent Van Goghs in oil. The street he lived in was called "Street of Peace - Friedensstraße" and i was over there at visiting my grandfather and grandmother every week, years long, when i got about twelve then i sat there the evening and just asked that one question : "Grandfather, have you been a Nazi ?" and from that on he never talked to me again, he was icy answering to me : "Yes, i was."

That other grandfather was violin teacher in GDR, and his wife was playing piano and loved languages. What can i say, that felt in a family often to be held like a stick of icecream in the frigde, they had not such a huge tolerance and attention to kids, we had to function, and i was most time outside and learned to grow from others.

Wrong Brothers ! Against commerce, only butt-fuckery,
fingers in the bum, Infantino, we shouldn't kill football,
we play naked and stretch ourselves out, whether we're men or women,
we show our balls, don't give a number, every document says that we didn't
stay friends, to those who ask for money for a number, if a fraudster says to
me, I'm going to throw money into our relationship,
then that's not my club, and I say "no", don't go into the forest,
and listen to the screaming of those who just turn the corner,
and want to conquer art for themselves, get my rights for themselves,
cook up false names with the brothers, give women false slips of the tongue.

I am just starting a novel, meanwhile almost two in one time, how ever long that takes, that one idea might be good really ! from now on i can't get that picture out of my head, see my jobcenter boss there asit with golden teeth from the earrings that i have to pay, still wait for the payment for a painting 100 € and wait for the publisher payment of the 107 €, had given the jobcenter the earnings then i keep from it 30 €.

Now one other Mister" Iwan Thieme "from Ukraine is comedian tells proudly presents himself as a new german citizan, after 6 years files and files and files. My own uncle from the time of GDR over there was called Iwan Thieme. I have a really widespread name, like sandcorn on the beach.

Like a german woman i made just the experience being a true heart, that never got the chance to a working contract, truth is unwanted, they abuse our womens rights with the socalled training of rhetorical traps manipulation bully and fake tellers, and at the last end if you won't stand the missionation of the A-hole then you stand alone, unemployed, ignored, and you might invite them for your reading and not more than five six people who appear, then blowing up the cheeks when i so won't greet them anymore, because i need none slick over my mouth when not want it by heart. I expect to be invited the future, or the things go wrong in future with us, all that what i know for sure it is not the truth of all people in the world, but if those A-holes alltogether just had the AIM to fight me, with the AIM to win over me, then they won't have a damn to do with me, who may believe in peace.

The stupid in Europe always think the same stupidity, that the white european woman is such a silly chick to make her in marriage pretty fast fat, and laugh about her, who had no professional chance, as if she would fit to that level living in a camping waggon to just wait the whole night long how devil sneaks around until she had to fight with, the times still have not changed for women here, but i am far too old to change backwards in times when i was seventeen to finally bring them the stupid chick, that i never have been. But i will care for your word, that it is worthier to keep my money until things like novels will be written, this might be pretty realistic. I AM NOT THE CHICK THAT BELONGS INTO THE SOUP !

Like i can remember that young comedian with the german passport now, he is called like my old uncle from GDR, too. My own uncle from the time of GDR over there was called Iwan Thieme, he died of cancer, uhh he was a huge cigar smoker all the way through ! His motherly name was Kosack.

125

You know the Kosack usually is one from Kasachstan in fromer times, with their pride on horseback, so we directly visited a farm from family when they directly put me on a horseback to go for a walk, and later on it was my wish to work and help in a horse stable in order to ride horses, and got to know the whole world of horse people in my town widespread, those who were Horse breeder, rider, private owner, hunter, veterinarian, helped out everywhere and was witness to a funeral for one old veterinarian, the person, who was often in our stable in lifetime, his horse was HUGE and had a back and form like a swan very funny, when i sat on this one, felt like a sofa and sink in it very comfortably, and also at a horse-drawn carriage wedding in the city, I was asked to bring the bride her flowers.

What i loved was the smell everywhere even the farrier. As very young child i visited that horse stable a few of times, when there lived a Mascot Goat, he stood always in the way and tried to make me afraid by staring at me, but i was not afraid, i messed with him. You know it was that smell of the veterinarian horse medicine in his tiny cupboard place where i had a look in it, the leather fat the liquor for the horse feet, the camphor essential oil, sothat it was easy to me to fold out the thought later on to become a physiotherapist, in order to be taught in anatomic medicine with my hands and empathy a practical healing with therapy most with water and massage. There, during my training, I became aware of the miracle of realignment, and one of my training partners became pregnant during the training and I massaged her until the baby came; that was a wonderful experience.

I mean i had more the trouble to flee my father afterwards, and to dive under to escape him, so that profession was fast forgotten. Don't be the keeper of everything There are things to let go of and things to finish. Enjoy the changing conditions because freedom is a feeling.

Good evening back my friend, I talked about our friendship to a single good old friend from the town to the danish border, who came along for coffee and cake. He was almost the adopting father to my alone raised child. He is old now and it is seldom see him, because now he started with a slightly dementia, and still drives his car. So we spoke about our both friendship.

You and Me, and what you teach me in human understandig of accepting lonelihood and letting things go, to realize self love and the acceptance of the other, and lovely human thoughts you gave me. His best friends is still his long years family from Tunesia. We are all holding together in all difficult times. It is and was our own reliable friendship of someone here in the north since more than 25 years, and because in younger years as social worker, educating in a youth home for school kids after school, he did lead the one 40 years long, his vacancy travels were often to North Africa, so I wrote him one novel once about an old man, on his travel in North Africa by bycicle and on his way back to turn to a monastery, in talk to a wise nun, and then decided to retire from then. But Arne always was in work to do, around his house and still those kids he cared in the tennisclub, so he never read it. Can't tell where they are coming from, because i did not in real meet his friends who live in his town, but anyway we cared for each other. Norma the family mom gave me spontaneously a few wonderful plates handmade and painted. I too collected such plates before. Now i have some wonderful collection, these are lovely plates, who did not break until today Not our friend is from Tunesia, but his friends that family who immigrated many years ago, if you meant Arne's Tunesian friends, who knows, i don't know, just knowing that his father that german one, was communist in WWII and fought strong as he could against Nazis, and then they killed him, sended him at last to join the war as canon food. That i didn't marry until today, it is just because i never had a partner before, yeah i often dreamed of Jews from the Nazi time, see them in gas chambers, see them dead lying around in the street, they are real nightmares, i feel it when these unexcepted folks do what they can to keep together or strive in life, they altime kinda paranoid, so they had to be the best in all they were doing, for me it is quiet better to be not Jewish, i had seen enough in my own life, what ever max nix may everybody become happy. If a friend is a good thinker, i say, you are kinda very tolerant young in heart, brilliant in wording, and like you said it a flying bird, that enjoys the wind, that is kinda pure innocence, that migh be disturbed by me at your side, because i am more experienced and not so innocent, that i am that lady fitting to you, you need an unbroken heart, with warmth and steady good mood, and a longing that brings you up to the moon, you need not to try to soften a bigger sister, i cannot change to innocent. Someone is welcome as friend, yes, as long as you return happy to where you live, and maybe want to come back once again, because you loved it.

Filling out certificates for strangers is out of the question. The last time I tried to ask for something online, I only asked for my ID details and 300 euros for nothing. The pretended friendship was a bluff. It's a shame sometimes, like this year when the famous strawberry June full moon was only hidden behind a long band of clouds. No, it was actually 3000 euros. And then the next person who chatted me up asked for the same amount, a full 3000 euros for nothing. And again, someone wanted to introduce himself as a nice Spaniard, and I noticed that he doesn't speak any Spanish. When I offered him something in Spanish, he immediately blocked me. So this time, no request for 3000 euros, hahahaha, so from now on our acquaintance is based on the payment of a sum on my part?

He might say: "The dog said to the wolf: "Who are you?" He said to him: "I am a friend of the lion." I say: "Wolf sat on the floor and was awakened by the light when he realized that the dog was his mother who was asking him for help."

Nonsense, I'm not asking for money, I hope you aren't either, I just read a certificate can mean anything, I'm not a bank; my bank advisor would hang me if I asked him for a loan for something dubious again, but it's good that he knows better and tells me that it's an extremely common scam. "When you sit with the lion and aren't allowed to talk about the mouse." Perhaps I'm being very clear and precise about that, but how else could it work? I haven't done anything wrong in our time together. My only great deed today was to forgive myself and my family, and to have written a pretty well-rounded, beautiful basic idea for the book. Oh well, I'm watching again how easy it is for you guys to make fun of people, ok before someone starts with the usual spiel and leaves me with a really big feeling of guilt. I'm afraid I have to step back for today, "

Then your victory in the fight against me was no right to prove that the "nice Europeans" are all basically being fooled, I don't regret anything." From my side i treated you upright with the respect as usual. But then looking back and seeing me as a sister isn't necessary, don't bother, I can manage on my own, so now it's good, first you shoot me down, then you ask again, there's no need for that. I just see you as far away, and you just took advantage of the situation, as is usual online, to abuse my trust, and by the way there is a saying: "Nice is the little sister of shit!" Are you still "acting like a lion"? I said at the beginning that you are too massive and powerful for me as a whole guy, and I am the only one who decides for myself. It annoys me, so I'm turning this conversation off. You have rules in life, so stick to them. I see that there are no recreational gangsters. The network is beyond measure a haven for liars !

We don't care who you are or whose son you are. We respect those who respect us and the rest doesn't matter. No one owes the other an apology, see you tomorrow. I just have a very bad idea now how it would be possible for a woman to share an apartment with a man, first sex, then a committed relationship, then no more small talk, and the woman is simply used for housework and definitely sent to the kitchen. That wouldn't be my problem. I'm not suggesting that other people's relationships don't work, but it is and will probably not be my problem.

We don't care who you are or whose son you are. We respect those who respect us and the rest doesn't matter. No one owes the other an apology, see you tomorrow. I just have a very bad idea now how it would be possible for a woman to share an apartment with a man, first sex, then a committed relationship, then no more small talk, and the woman is simply used for housework and definitely sent to the kitchen. That wouldn't be my problem. I'm not suggesting that other people's relationships don't work, but it is and will probably not be my problem.

There is no safety and there is no end...
 the word must be heard, in silence, there must be darkness to see the stars..
...there must be no end to fully understand what is forever...there must be
darkness to be able to see who you really are...there must be chaos to fully
understand it's consequences...

We remain an enigma in this life We are the ones whose features show
nothing but calmness. We are the ones who turn to no one when we are sad.
We heal ourselves no matter how painful we are. We are the ones who do
not surrender to the bitterness of the days, we accept everything that
happens silently and then go on our way in peace. And peace to our souls
when peace is lacking in our lives. The days were the same, the people were
the same, so we did not care who stayed and who left. The faces around us,
the relationships, the feelings, even the pains, shocks and disappointments
were similar in us, but we began to expect them at all times and from every
person, no matter how high his position in our hearts. Our feelings were
similar, so laughter replaced tears, our misery and our lamentations. When
joy overcame us, lost amidst similarities, we did not recognize them all, we
were not attracted to any of them, nor did we feel repelled. It has erased
every pleasure, taken away every pleasure, killed every desire and thwarted
every attempt.

Don't try to recalculate yesterday and what you lost in it. Once the leaves
fall, they don't come back. But with each new spring, other leaves grow, so
look at the leaves that cover the sky. Forget what falls to the ground, it has
become a part of it.

Never trust the same person who hurt you again.

Nature doesn't change. Life is painful when it shocks you with what you
thought was good. Compliment those who come to you in their free time.
Appreciate the one who gives you your free time. And hold on to the one
who pretends to be you...

Don't trust everything you see, even salt looks like sugar...

Be who you are, don't pretend. Whoever wants you will love you as you are, with your flaws. Be yourself, everyone has a story and ending...

Don't be too sure of your place in people's hearts.
People wake up with different feelings every day... Their attitude is constantly changing and their emotions fluctuate in an instant. They can leave you for the most trivial reason and you may be replaced by others.

People are stages, not houses. One stage may last longer than the other. But in the end, you will return home alone...

Don't trust anyone...... Even the dust you were created from will bury you one day...

I met you here and, in the humorous situation, you were my first lifesaver! Your way of expressing things finally showed me that a man is also a thinker who can do magic. Your work with or on people, in my example, has reinforced the statement that living alone is possible, if only to understand one's life, which is not possible otherwise. I finally feel like a normal part of society, without being judged for it because people are, on average, jealous. I would often have broken down out of pride because of my waterfalls of tears and moments of sadness; for me, that lasted for 40 years. And it is exactly as you say, laughter, it actually accompanies you throughout your whole life. It calms you down the more you learn about being human. Since I have known you, when I laugh, I no longer fall into the void in which the people around me are all just one piece of water, blurring together, but I see more than ever that the light shines through between all people.

Be aware of what I owe you! You have not succumbed to the drug of life. I finally know the meaning of flying !

The art of living has a title...
Don't save anything for later.
Later the coffee gets cold.
Later you lose interest.
Later the day turns into night.
Later people grow up.
And later life passes...
And then you regret not doing something.
When you get the chance...
Life is a fleeting dance, a delicate balance of moments unfolding before us, never the same again. Regret is a bitter pill to swallow, a burden that weighs on the soul with the weight of missed opportunities and unspoken words. So let's not put anything off for later. Let's seize the moments to come with open hearts and outstretched arms to seize the opportunities that await us. Because in the end, it's not the things we did that we regret, but the things we left undone, the words we didn't say, and the dreams unfulfilled.

Have a wonderful day!

Yes, we see so many opportunities that the animal perceives with such passion. The rabbit always runs towards me on the street at midnight because he loves running along it! The ferret likes to go between the houses in the early evening hours to walk under the cars in parking lots. The deer family always crosses the paths together on the circular path in the same places, and then they almost step on my feet. The stubborn loner roebuck speaks to me loudly and still recognizes me seven years later on his paths, he always stands almost on the paths where people see him standing quietly and fascinates everyone because he is fearless and complains loudly when necessary. The eagle throws himself headlong into love so exuberantly that you would think he started to go crazy until his recklessness became his undoing and females cried for a year after losing them. If we had never taken the path to nature, where would people belong, in the toilet at the train station? Even the tiny blue kingfisher flies out behind the hills whenever I come, shooting from the tree on the left across the meadow to the pond opposite. The heron in the small forest swamp sits up there, and if you just stand there and wait a few minutes, it can fly over your head. You just walk a little way in the woods and five meters further on there is a real eagle sitting on the ground in front of you. I don't want paths that only go around houses, in a nice round curve, past benches and garbage cans where dogs can't run. There are four directions, all of which lead to a little paradise if you just walk long enough! Have a nice evening at home too !

American everyday life is designed for the winning side, the shadow does not exist for them. You always see Americans turning up in huge numbers, there is always shouting, vying for attention, alcohol and fast food are also given out for free for advertising purposes so that the party gets voted for, everything according to the motto "Everything - Everywhere - and Immediately!" One critical look or well-considered statement and you make an enemy. Have you ever imagined a little boy in a soccer uniform who likes to practice his soccer ball in the middle of the night on the front lawn or a little girl who, regardless of embarrassment, goes for a pee on the lawn in front of the house? That doesn't exist in the USA, it's almost against the law.

The latest Western threat!
The "progress" of the "West" soon a faint memory...!
I remember, when my child was small, I could fill my shopping cart
for 2 weeks' shopping for 50 Deutschmarks.
10 years later the Euro came along,
and then you could only get half the goods for 50 euros.
20 years later today, for 50 euros you can only get basic bread, sausage,
cheese, toilet paper, milk and coffee, maybe vegetables from the market,
and that's it! And then America wants to make the brilliant suggestion
that we Europeans would....no longer trade with them,
and that tariffs would prevent any sales ! We could hear the flutter miles
away, when hundreds of birds flapped their wings and flew
in fascinating formations, when the air was clean and sky pristine
decades ago, now it's only stories, and memories
of melodic lines, and chorus of birdsong.

That's for your information! Don't make any effort.
As if you were interested in the "niceness" of European women,
whose mothers only cook with water,
whose fathers recently washed the dishes,
whose children see no future for their pensions.
German women in % only have 1 child, if at all,
millions of people are leaving the church because of abuse,
politics is not child-friendly, traffic is not pedestrian-friendly,
education is not... adapted to new conditions.

If you had ever shown true commitment to the well-being of our born
children, ... instead of taking after us early on, who knows?

Is there a basic right to clean drinking water?
But in fact 1000 children under 5 die EVERY DAY from unclean water,
in cities with ostentatious construction mania, which city TODAY
invests in water treatment to prevent dying rivers?
Perhaps one in all of Europe !

Hadrian's Wall,
a Roman-designed border wall to Scotland,
a joke, 117 kilometers long,
lies in the middle of England,
in dry peat bogs,
rotting when water accumulates,
disappearing in preservation.

The Danevirke Wall,
a Viking-designed border wall
to northern Germany, a joke,
15 meters long, the rest of it
lies by the side of the road in dry sand,
far from the old days, the pubs rot,
the parts of the wall that are lost during the tourist boom.

Once the accordion has been opened, it should never be able to close again! It is like the numerous opportunities in life to tackle something, to say something, to admit regret about your own mistakes, to even ask for forgiveness. If you instead keep all these moments to yourself without consent, you will not pass the test of having always acted correctly! It does not depend on the things you have done, but much more on not letting the coffee get cold and taking significant actions, not letting the undone actions lie around, which may make you seem grown-up, but having lived past them until you have the chance to make up for it all is a waste of time! A short life is wasted. The saying still applies: "If someone has done bad things to you, never approach them again in your life!" because it is far too much trust to simply assume that others will treat you with dignity and honesty, or reciprocate what you feel in the same way. When you met them, they were only reflected in your ability to love, but the same did not come from them.

I look at them, the ones that happen outside, the woman as a fat woman, left me standing on her bike, that her figure is not that of a lady, not even that of a woman, her figure is more like the imitation of a male figure, perhaps of her father, or they walk ashamed at the side of a man who, despite her contempt for the woman of her own self, always takes her by the hand like a father, the massive contempt of a woman who always remained a little girl, and even this form shows no movement of her hips that says she has ever really lived out her desires or learned something from life. Every day that passes becomes a realization for you, which I can see for myself here far away.

No matter how much you serve some people and how much you sacrifice for them, do not expect gratitude from them... and no matter what you do for them, one day it will be worth nothing in their eyes. Sometimes you are selfish and give them the rest first. No matter what you do for them, you miss them, even if there is fire and light in you, and if you build hills for them, over the hills of love... you are still wrong. If you spend your life doing this, they will inevitably shock you.

This is how some people are, no matter what you do, you will remain humanly negligent towards them. There are people, no matter what you do for them, for them your actions remain a point on the sidelines. Such a person one day denies your favor and kindness as if you had done nothing, and when he regains his strength, you find that he is ungrateful for everything and stays away from you, and accuse them of being negligent because their most important interests are over and they want more from you without acknowledging what you did before. They needed you and when they got up and recovered, they hated everything you did. But we say: Praise be to God who has implanted mercy in us. He has made us a reason to help those who need us, our origins and humanity, which is no longer present in most people.

They see their own mistakes as mountains that are difficult to carry. Stay away from them, because no matter Whatever you do, you will not reach an agreement with them.

My advice is always be cynical. That way you will never be disappointed. That saying "That in Europe it is mainstream, that those parents and people in many ways abuse their children !"meant otherwise us Mothers saying, "That give birth to children, is still Not - the invention - of those Mother and Child abusers !"

It should be admitted that the intolerable imposition that America's natives are subjected to by immigrants like Trump... that he should have refrained from doing this earlier, at the beginning of the wave of emigration, by taking a cruise to the West. It would have had far less serious consequences. And today, born here in Kaiserslautern, today's Little America City, he would be of no use for anything else and would be playing groundskeeper for the football club!!! If the Crusaders had never existed, we would all have been spared !

My friend, the hero. First he pretended to be Helene Fischer!
My friend, look at him especially since he was playing
the role of Sponshbob today and threw me out of bed with a neigh!
My friend, you're kidding, then he plays the role of the drunk mother
who insults me so much that I'm lying in the corner depressed !
My friend, you've got it, that's why I'd better not look
in the mirror in your presence, who knows what will happen next?

I think that strange men on the networks,
all of them actually just comparatively like fakes or bot characters,
act towards women like fare dodgers, all live in their own little BUBBLE,
never able to escape from it, and I always just watch
how long their job as a "fare dodger" will last !

Do you wanna know how the pimp is in mind ?
A strange day.
Life can sometimes play tricks on a man. He wanders among his peers for far too long in search of love, even before he remembers who he is. It's like he's living a double life, playing the role of the well-adjusted, loyal family man on the one hand, and in the other life with someone else, trying to fulfill himself, playing his second role in parallel, always there for everyone at the same time, but far removed from the one who lives inside him.

Everything that goes on around him is information from the left, just as much information from the right, and the poor man can't tell the difference between the fact that most of the statements that reach him are always more or less based on the truth of one side or the other.
That's why men often come to the realization, even at a young age, that the severed head of a lizard could definitely grow back, like its tail, maybe even one of its arms and legs, just because someone somewhere in this universe said that.

So it happens that one day this man finds himself in a situation that is almost hopeless, and fate once again awakens in him the revival of his view of the world, which is his experience in connection with reality and how everything fits together. It seems to him like a hammer blow from Thor, and the wise insight to understand his life!

He is exposed as a fare dodger. His method of getting to know random, friendly women is to tell them witty stories, to flatter them, to gain their favor, to trust and desire for them directly, to give them tasteless compliments, to act like a fundamental moral thinker, to start from his own helpless situation, and suddenly to juggle with high numbers again, as if there was no other way and not that he was the one who "paid" the women. But until he can successfully "take the fish off the hook" and "soften up" the woman for his own amusement, he throws her a few philosophical morsels now and again to cover up his actual personal hardness, strength and coldness.

138

To make an impression, in repeated devaluations still remorsefully asking for help on how he should behave better in her eyes?

So that the old woman can feel important again.

But actually admitting that he sends his mother into the kitchen herself, who is allowed to prepare his meals every day, prefers to sleep during the day and roam around at night and stay awake, just like a leaf in the wind, until the leaf lies on the ground afterwards and becomes earth again, for someone like him, relationships with people are like mayflies that last as long as the sun shines in the sky, but will fade away again when the weather turns bad. Making a baby for a woman, but first soaking her in a test tube of his feelings, the chemistry of their relationship being more like that of a Neanderthal, giving his sister the cold shoulder, accusing his neighbor of leaving him alone, fooling intellectual women into believing that they are just about adorable for their age, setting priorities differently when women imagine they find a friend in him, not granting the woman wisdom, denying that she probably has no maternal connection to life because her mother has never repented and therefore never seen a real light dawn on her in her entire existence, and in the form of her dog she did not recognize the presence of her ancestors. He devalues the woman's dog. In his opinion, it is always the look from the wall of an owl, like the eyes of his mother watching over him, that he does not commit himself seriously to a woman, as the only remaining son who does not leave her, and that is why the attractive woman has been degraded to him by him to be a sick pussy. The wolf he wants to be, the lion he pretends to be, in reality the lapdog he is for his mother. His deepest wish and desire is to use social networks to take other impressive women and mothers into his confidence in order to teach them about someone else's life and thereby take away their pride, because this is his game, as it is so superficial and anonymous in this swamp of dating, no one can stop misogynistic men from behaving deceitfully and harming others.

My advice is to always be cynical. That way you will never be disappointed.

We can't stop the waves, but we can learn to swim.
This life teaches patience, not every day is wonderful...
and our lives are not always what we want...
This is life... it carries many fates within it.
A dream comes true... and a dream stumbles... a meeting without a date...
and a separation without a reason...Neither the beginnings you expect...
nor the endings we want. And life goes on...

Patience for me is staying alive on the edge.
The unexpected happens when you make strangers into friends.
What we know is what others want. What others want is not good for them.
A meeting without a date may be someone else's moment of enlightenment.
A dream only comes true when you stop stumbling.
The stumbling dream is like an upside-down cigarette
in front of the camper van, and calling this a vacation,
which is recognizable after absolute loneliness nonsense.
Life has a back as long as a dog's. And in the end it's always his cock.

How many people have we lost in our lives because we were too real and
honest in all the things we offered?

We have lost because we were unable to fake our feelings and embellish the
way we dealt with them.

We were unable to be sincere and open. We do not know how to twist
ourselves or take on a character that contradicts our personality. We do not
know hypocrisy, politeness and resistance to our beliefs and principles.

We have lost because we have not offered anything except from our depths,
because we only care about being ourselves. We have lost a lot, but we have
gained ourselves, and that is the most important gain in our lives.

But what happens when people are constantly searching and are worn out in
drought, and when they pray for rain, are they never safe from the storm?

I let my father live his life as he sees fit. He doesn't have long anymore anyway. To deny an old man an evening like this would be a crime, and it could also be that I was the person in his life on whom he acted out his sadism. As an old man, all he has left today is a pitiful legacy of the handful of shabby people around him who put up with him because they themselves don't care about life any more than their noses. I know that in about ten years almost all of those he calls his generation of accomplices, who supported a criminal, will no longer be here. Then there will be no one left of the entire family that I knew. I have already made real inner peace. They will have no more than one last ugly thought, and then they will be no more.

It is said that an Italian artist painted his painting and considered it the most beautiful of all... Therefore, he wanted to challenge everyone with it, so he placed it in a public place and wrote the following sentence over it: ((Whoever sees a defect, even a very simple one, should put a red sign over it)).

When he returned in the evening, he found that it was distorted, with red signs here and there indicating a defect, so that the original painting was completely obscured by the red circles. He went to his teacher and decided to stop drawing because his drawings were so bad. The teacher told him to just change the sentence, and he drew the same painting and placed it in the same place, but he painted colors and a brush and wrote under it the following sentence:

(Whoever sees a defect, even a very simple one, should take up the pen and quill and fix it.)) Until the evening, no one approached the painting, so he left it for days and no one approached it. The teacher said to him: - Son, have you seen? Many people see the fault in everything... but the fixers are rare...

Dear reader
This is the state of people in our world today!! Our shameful reality is that we only see faults, we love to criticize and belittle this and that, but no one offers solutions... and this is due to a lack of love. We do not love each other and do not wish for anything well and success, so never be one of those.. May God bless your time with happiness.

as if it weren't one mistake after another that we have to see, as if our human life was a painting in which each of its mistakes is highlighted in red and then suddenly falls off the wall? But who could endure being alone within these four walls and following this long corridor through all its corridors until they find it, their self? And how can anyone today still endure sending out this self in their head or heart or chest as a pleasant feeling that can be detected at rest?

No more critics, no more morals, no more egoists who are important to everyone! I know the way in which people on the run seek help locked in train carriages, get no water, breathe no air, spend too long inside, let families die in them! Even politicians use refugees to increase the pressure on others, we don't board trains these days that transport people to camps, it happens on land, on water, in the air! Humanity today is worth nothing !

Yay, what kind of motley group of people are you traveling with now? Is it worth asking, or has someone annoyed you recently? What experience can you tell us about someone who is going on a trip...? What languages have you been speaking recently? Can you afford the tobacco, what you like to drink? Will we see each other again this year? If the number of strangers who are assholes is as high as that of our German neighbors.

How do you deal with it? I guess you'll move. Do the nights still get long in the beautiful summer? Now that cold days alternate with warm ones all year round, do you still love swimming outside? With all your skills, being such a language talent and being studied scientist, you're a survival pro, it's a shame that I didn't get to do that like you did. I've always wanted to visit North Africa myself, even as a woman. But as we know, it's dangerous for inexperienced men, too, in your continent. So I travel in my imagination like I always do in life. There is still plenty of room for travel, and I will never grow up because I don't give a damn about adults.....

blessings, Heike !

Drinking in the afternoon,
while other people go to work,
then you go to bed in the morning,
then you can start all over again,
in the West they have a stick up their ass,
the little man's sunshine, are fucking and being drunk,
affirming life in epidemics, alcohol you evil spirit,
you threw my dad down the drain, now you want me, get out of here !
Can it be vegan sausage?
Go ask over there on the other meadow.
There could be more victims like you,
it comes as it comes, good luck, you sausage !

We've just run out of meat.
And we'll have to pound a schnitzel onto a vegan roast first.
A joke like "Punch the Lukas" is not wanted,
you can also send him to his death with "stroking".
If you can't stand a joke, you don't like to admit that everyone has disliked
each other at some point, that they were great at bullying each other,
that criticism of everything is the usual way of ruining things for others,
complaining in itself is like the bacterial culture in fried sauerkraut,
that you only keep yelling at others as long as you do,
because it will only make you feel better, that everyone understands,
people are good at that, because the suffering of others is good for you,
whoever dishes things out still feels himself, he is alive,
and determines what is human only for himself,
so whoever wants something, whatever it is, can pull you over.
The wolf asit on the floor in awareness of the light. That dog aside enters the
room as his mother apologize. The dog asks the Wolf "Who are you ?"
the Wolf answered "I am the friend of the Lion !" - Heike Thieme -

Always be careful of the tempting distance. Travelling alone in Africa
would mean not only being attacked with brutality, but also getting to know
the dangerous animals and standing in a vast field, often without water in an
emergency. These three things in the south are life-threatening, which can
happen if no emergency help arrives by chance. In the north, wilderness is
always romantically considered to be the adventure option, which is also
underestimated, because staying in the wilderness is associated with the
same risks that people usually overestimate themselves for beforehand,
because they always want to do it "alone" as heroes. I'm telling you, even in
the Californian desert, in Arizona itself, people go to the dogs as refugees,
so to proudly talk about all the great experiences you've had out in the open
is a bit overly vain in my opinion, you can just clap your mountain bike next
to the refugees with a bottle of water under your arm and tell everyone
afterwards what you can do! So why not ride your bike to Iraq, Tibet,
Ethiopia or Afghanistan and back, being fed by all the locals along the way,
squeezing into their houses and feeling like a hero, and maybe even having

your photo taken in good spirits alongside the convoys of refugees all over the world, squeezing past and getting help out of every stupid situation you find yourself in as a paying tourist?

It is not always the distance that matters, but also how far one has learned to experience oneself in silence and to endure the shock of this self-knowledge without judging it. Have fun, I don't want to spoil it for you. I only had my uncle Ernst, the one from Berlin, he used to travel all over the world on his own. And he told me terrible things about Africa. Of course he never agreed with this civilization either, but more from the point of view that the indigenous people and the animal world are dying out. He has been living with his sister for a long time in their adopted home of Copenhagen. They can't even stand the Germans anymore. That's why I say yes, I got to know the family from all sides of the world, north, south, east and west, but I, the only person who had to go through everything, was not liked or welcomed by any of these related families, or could have claimed to expect help from them. That's why I, like you, always prefer people from far away. Best wishes, and take good care of yourself, I would love to see you again in one piece!

I feel the same way. But I also think highly of the indigenous people, who today still live in caves in Africa like in the Stone Age. They really do know everything about us humans. And that's why, when I reach certain personal maturity levels, I dream of these people who praise me for my insight, the women of the high council. They are simply everywhere, but not many people notice them today. People reduce their brain mass, they change their physical constitution with environmental toxins, they misjudge reality for what it is. For so long, they are stuck in a dream bubble that is guaranteed not to save them from any situation in case of danger, but they don't know that. I won't let myself be dragged into any more mulchy church, I'm just not responsive to such slips of the tongue and seduction. It always had a stale, unpleasant aftertaste to have to deal with people like that,

NO THANKS!

The indigenous are living their thoughts
and the 'civilised' are trying to figure out
their big secrets to profit on,
it must always be the big mystery and
complication otherwise all our science and
technology has to be a hoax if you really can
live without it...
like having all facts and numbers
about the date, otherwise it won't be 'the
ultimate match', but that produced mass
of technologized wording chaos,
won't bring them further.
This is only the idea of it.
But one single seemingly idea
that is not concrete,
it a full fupp at the end of the day.

Written by the poet Ahmed Matar*

The story of a donkey, the son of a donkey, is very beautiful

Once upon a time there was a group of donkeys in one of the Arab stables. One day a donkey went on a hunger strike for some time. His body became weak, his ears drooped, and his body almost fell to the ground from weakness. The donkey father noticed that his son's condition was getting worse day by day. He wanted him to understand the reason for this. He came to him alone to examine his increasingly deteriorating mental and health condition.

He said to him: What's wrong with you, my son? I brought you the best varieties of barley... and you still refuse to eat...Tell me, what's wrong with you? Why are you doing this to yourself? Was someone bothering you?

The donkey's son raised his head and turned to his father:
Yes, father... they are people...
The donkey father was amazed and said to his little son:
What is wrong with people, my son?
He said to him: They make fun of us donkeys.
The father said: How is that?
The son said: "Don't you see that every time someone commits a shameful act, they say to him: 'You donkey...'

And whenever one of their children commits a vice, they say to him: 'You donkey.' Are we really like that? They describe their idiots as donkeys... and that is not how we are, father...We work tirelessly. We understand and understand.

Then the donkey father was confused and did not know how to answer his little one's questions while he was in this bad state. But he quickly moved his ears left and right, then he began to converse with his son, trying to convince him according to the logic of donkeys.

Look, my son, they are a group of people, God created them and preferred them over all other creatures, but they did a lot of harm to themselves before offending us, the donkeys.

*See for example. In all your life, have you seen a donkey stealing his brother's money?? Have you heard of this?

*Have you seen a donkey torturing other donkeys for no other reason than because they were weaker than him or because he didn't like what they said?

Have you seen a racist donkey treating other donkeys with racism in terms of color, gender and language?

Have you heard of the summit of donkeys who don't know why they have gathered?

Have you ever heard that American donkeys are planning to kill Arab donkeys!! To get barley?

Have you seen a donkey who is an agent of a foreign country and conspired against the donkeys of his country?

Have you seen a donkey separated from his family for sectarian reasons?

Of course, in the world of donkeys, you have never heard of such human crimes!!

But do people know the wisdom of their creation and act well according to it? Therefore, my son, I ask you to control your donkey mind. I ask you to hold up my head and your mother's head. And you remain, as I promised you, *a donkey, son of a donkey*,,

And let them, my son, say what they want. *It is enough for us to be proud that we are donkeys*

We do not lie
We do not kill
We do not steal
We do not gossip
Do not swear
We do not dance for joy as long as there are wounded and dead among us.

The son was impressed by these words, so he got up and began to devour the barley and said: "Yes, I will remain as you promised me, father.. I will continue to be proud that I am a *donkey, son of a donkey*. Then I will be dust and will not go into the fire whose fuel is people and stones.

Young people of today, such "upstarts", am I not alone in asking myself,
why are you standing here in a suit that you don't even fit into?
You are young at heart, where would you actually be
if not travelling through India with a backpack?
Is that how you want to prepare me for what life without work is like?
I know, yes, there are certain things that none of us can see,
but that will come our way anyway,
without us knowing about them beforehand.
So two young men in ties wanted to impress upon me the "truth,"
that they knew how things could be better in the future?

We scan the circle, what,
as a university graduate and pop hairstyle?
With regard to our weaker members of the group,
those with difficult childhoods,
those with an abandoned life partnership,
those with a place to sleep in the car as an escape in the crisis,
how does the financial world react to this in the test?

Have we all brains of Birds ? Because most of us humans, want to live without relationship, and fear that so much to stay single the whole damn life ?

Look sideways
disguised dominance
to go to great

In dressing Ambition
the words
gives religious respect

Be a philanthropist
trade in being human
what friendship remains a trade

Navel policy
compensates loveless
gain self-love

Maternal instinct
mother animal served
to subjugate others

Perhaps freed from suffering
prediction of misfortune
own life

No soil
inventing self-love
to attract trust

Great mind
only a noble profile
to get praise

Iron heart is flattery
as a result
in circulation to vanity

Always ready for violence
virtue loses itself
like rivers in the sea

Always high
to honor the vices
poison has a healing effect

The stairs to the lake
the mountain at the end
eyes that obey

Shift, fourth gear
drunk in love
healthy from fever

Truly a withdrawal
darkness turns out
what love was

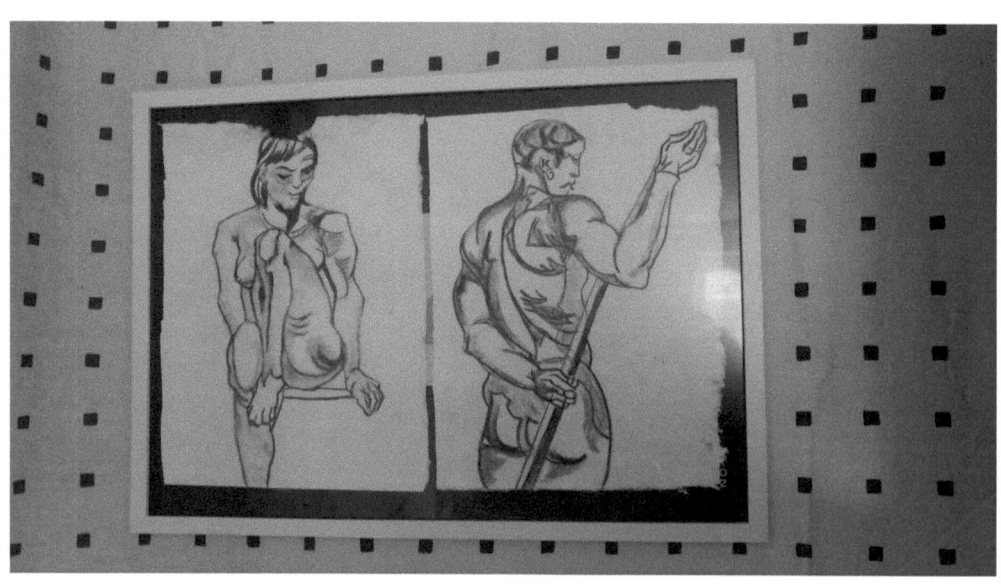

Isn't that funny? I trust you more like an older, mature, wise man, a well-educated man, whom I never knew for long, whom I haven't known for as long as you guys, younger friends I've been chatting with for six years! I suppose the word "older" annoys you, so I'll explain to you that in my way of dealing with people, almost every deep conversation with exceptions was with younger men, who I initially found sweet and nice, but all of them are having a lot of fun, pretending to be more amazing, experienced, artistic, passionate, well-traveled and cosmopolitan, but when things turn out, every time it turns out that they know nothing, don't get to know people who are not well or who really need help, and in these cases they don't even recognize others outside themselves as needy. 90% of people are show-offs and profiteers, people with pretenses who make crude and unfair jokes about others, ignore them and can be quite cruel. That's why I really and truly associate the word "older" with a wonderful quality of people who communicate and write from a real background for what they say - a much nicer and more honest quality compared to the people who want to be the "eternal savages" but who, when you approach them, immediately slam the door in your face so hard that you see stars until you no longer feel the blood in your veins, who themselves have been "celebrated" with their sympathy for years. You wouldn't believe how many times I've seen the stars, probably as many times as you can count the stars in the sky, as if I should behave like those bio-aunts, the absolute oddballs, of Germans, with an abbreviation of all these variable conversations, and still only get laughter that at some point becomes unreal. I know what I learned was to confront myself in all directions and turns.

"A heart that wants and a mind that refuses, and a thousand battles in a body."

There is an eternal battle between mind and heart.
The human soul is perceived only by the Creator.
Do not test each other on this.
The conflict between mind and heart.
A battle that tires the soul. Between a heart that wants and a mind that refuses. A certain heart and mind tell it that they are illusions.

Between this and that, the soul is lost.
A heart that wants to fly away
and a mind that captivates it.
A heart lost in dreams, a mind that awakens it, and a soul that cries for help.
A battle in which you are the only loser.If the mind wins this battle, the heart dominates the soul, so dreams come to you in spectra that the heart desires, and when you wake up, you find that the mind laughs, the heart cries, and the soul is lost. And everything in between.

THEY CALL IT.... THE SMALL SECTS ARE GETTING A LITTLE TIME INTO IT,

IN THE STATE OF "SLEEPY HOLZBEIN" or "SCHLESWIG-HOLSTEIN" it sounded like STARTING A NEW EXPERIMENT, it's been going on for 35 YEARS!

Does the couple want to show how couples live together, then demonstrate to the audience, for a bit of piousness, make a group of "needy people" who are sent to them by the state work for free in a prayerful way, i.e. undergo a tiny little test to see how well they can be integrated into such "camps", the couple earn a good bit of money on the side, intimidate the critics and those around them and witnesses, who report this to the state, and then snoop on them a bit, talk the children out of it by reporting it to the authorities, i.e. cheekily denounce them for the criticism, and the newly born child is "GONE" so that the dear church can have peace again, and a lid on it, because no one dares to leave the church without the kick in the butt, into unemployment, which would be inevitable?
THE REST GOES WITH THE MOTTO – NITIFIATION!

"Die Magie der Märchen umsetzen fast unmöglich daran gesehen,
wie die Frauen in der Liebe scheitern, Lampe mit dem Inhalt ihrer Wünsche,
die an Ungleichheit und Desillusion scheitert,
Zittern lassen einen nicht die Träume, zittern der Frauen Ängste in Nächten,
jeder hat Träume im eigenen Leben, Unterschied wie 1000 und eine Nacht,
es gehen keine solche Leute einzusperren, Köpfe schwellen, schier platzen,
sich laut Verstand und Herz sich streiten, bis sich die Seele Freiheit schafft,
und sie erst erlöst sind, wenn sie ihr Recht zu erst auf deren eigenen Träume
zu zugehen, die Sehnsucht erst mal auf einen Baum hoch jagen, um sich den
Traum dann wie den Apfel mit beiden Händen runter pflücken !"

The magic of fairy tales is almost impossible
to implement, as can be seen how fail in love,
the lamp with the content of their wishes fails
because of inequality and disillusionment.
It is not dreams that make you tremble,
it is women's fears that make tremble at night.
Everyone has dreams in their own life
that are as different as 1001 nights.
It is not possible to lock people like that up
because their heads are swelling and almost
bursting, their minds and hearts argue loudly
until their souls create freedom, and they are
only released when they exercise their right to
first pursue their own dreams, to first chase
their longing up a tree, and then pick the
dream off with both hands like an apple!

Watering too late won't save the tree, hahaha, that could be true!
I see so many trees running around each other, and I've been friends with
them for 30 years, but they all doubt my integrity, so maybe they all had
something genuine for me just once, but then turned away from me forever
in disgust, and I see them age much earlier, to their detriment. See - life also
has its amusing side! hahaha and when I was a child, no one planted a tree
in my memory, but I created a small animal cemetery for lost and found
items of this kind, nobody could make me fear horses, because the more
often they threw me in the mud, the more often I got up afterwards, and
each time there was no pain involved ! Even as a child I saw that an old man
had to grow up before me his whole life like an old turned, carved, dark
piece of wood on which he leans, and yet does his work until he drops, and
he never says a word about it !

One of them, the little one, was told early on:
"Your mother didn't give a damn about you!"
but it was clearly a planned child removal
and the psychopath got his way.
Another one, her child was the means:
"You see how... my child is committing suicide!
I'll tell everyone how godless they all are!"
but it was staged, to instigate
the church's susceptibility to racism.
One of them learned at the age of 2
to recognize the philosopher in herself
that her silence lasted 50 years.
"She should be considered insane, negligent, irresponsible and ungrateful!"
but today, with almost five years of professional experience
as a philosopher, I say:
"I'm curious now, father, what will you have to tell me
when you break your silence after 50 years!"

The music has to play in the rain,
then the operetta can throw people
with bags of money onto the stage in a bathing suit,
so that its advertising revenue makes an impression,
the cover is overrun by the crowd,
the others should fight the floods,
for an hour of storm surge with concert noise,
just brings in a quick buck,
this also brings the ex-student
with a short event played in the rain
even more for just fake style, and no political statement,
recognizable as "political correctness"
for 50,000 fans, a good 13 million in the ladies' purse.

Dress Men, hostesse service manager,
muscles in suit, serious proposal advertisor,
event hall welcomes,
some call it for the callgirls'
Insider tip for organized rapists in the quarry field,
next to the lake,
on the edge of the bank,
on the gravel stone,
for professionals who are
above things like marriage....

We spend our lives looking for the keys to enter people who have no doors.
If the door to a person is only through his one eye,
which welcomed you as well as you admirably accept it,
then all you have to do is smile happily,
and one compliment turns to another!
Women don't fall in love like we do, my friend.
Women fall in love with money, power and influence.
I have never seen a woman in my life who was proud of her man because
he is loyal and honest or because he cares for her!

How many times have I looked at the one-eyed man?
How many times has he run away from me?
How many times has he honestly never liked me,
and yet always wants to be loved again?
How many names you bear as a man, that's what matters.
How many women you know, man, that's how you approach me.
How many times have I tried with you,
and then picked myself back together in small pieces.
What does that have to do with money and gold?

In contrast to supposedly... my big emotional problems,
which is why my child was stolen from me in bed with violence...hahahah,
I am an experienced horse groomer, was a prospective geriatric nurse,
had training as a physiotherapist, used my knowledge to support disabled,
created good artistic paintings, conveyed my social skills and
knowledge in 120 books, well, and as planned, I successfully
raised my child to be a self-confident, clear-headed person!
No matter now, I didn't become a missionary victim after all how this kind
of mission is translated can be discovered in any cemetery at any time !

I assume that
the man is almost impossible to save !
He looks like an American,
with a deep erotic voice,
alone in the fitness center like...
a piece of meat in the display !
It looks like the hysterical stalkcrs,
the supposed future mothers,
the wallflowers sent by dad,
who all spend their lives waiting on the dung heap,
for someone to finally free them,
were sent there for him!
I only advise him, "Don't make yourself part of the potato salad !"
You will bitterly regret it !

After the fall of the wall,
nobody cared at all,
try it out, it tastes light,
like strawberry & chocolate,
the chosen model child,
never has to work,
the bastard child, just has to slip up,
its anger drove it to flee,
until then it was persecuted by him,
even a bungler...needs his "pride",
he tells the story for the rest of his life !

It always goes so far, to be rejected by your father,
who only meets you with the flat of his hand in the face,
who considered me to be "his mistake",
who never felt like a daughter, but did everything to have a real "father",
Everything who locked me away for years,
called me insane, for the violence that was done to me,
Everything he tried to do, let me rot there,
NONE of it - NOTHING can be made right again!!
He was just waiting for the day to come
when he would take my child away from me and...
for the day to come when I "PUNISHED" MYSELF!!
I don't fly straight into someone's arms
when it comes to love, I don't need a quartet!
I'D RATHER MIGRATE TO A NEW PLANET!
TOMORROW THE WEATHER IS SUPPOSED TO BE BETTER AGAIN!

Passers-by who are quick to communicate...
I should approach them in a healthy way,
I should show everyone else scepticism,
I should take an example from them,
I should tell the graduates their motto,
I should get out of their way,
I should not get on anyone's nerves,
I should ask my ancestors what they tell me,
I should not approach them a second time,
I should fuck everyone to the moon and back,
I should show respect to the professionally trained teacher,
I should always show my smile,
I should never doubt, not even myself,
I should translate their regret as guilt,
I should interpret their rejection as unfortunately
not being able to make it in time,
I should pretend to be unconditionally interested in them,
I should stand with them in the middle of the rain,
I should act like a fool for the sake of the officials,
I should come crawling for love,
I should pretend to be a country girl,
I should block out their perverse desires,
I should first be abused, then serve in friendship,
I should always greet the little haters,
I should send little messages to stupidity,
I should enthusiastically call their descendants geniuses.

Had just finished the new book, but haven't got the money to publish, then waiting until next month, shall go and make that new title and the new cover, that makes fun, it is silently said, really my life essence in describing the psychopath in my father, and inside of another story, my essence, then the consequence to me and fazit to learn of it. It is wonderful spoken, if it was not ME who has lived that Life, then nobody would have found my PHILOSOPHER in me !
ohhh yesss it is one of the ones i wrote who are good advisors:

against the young girls fairy prince syndrom i wrote...
"Direction to future days"
against the women marriage complexity i wrote "Ask the jelly fish"
against the abusive politic for ex. in USA i wrote a solidarity book
"Loyality" dedicated to someone in OHIO
one next english version shows short cutted the image to bear the worst in stay positive, to carry life along in a positive way, like i do, still no title
ahh against the abuse in online proposals, to make aggressive business on good believers with lies and fraud, i wrote the book
"Careful with the Dating trap "

......then i have got 120 books !

no, you see it real, the most won't pay with money anymore, the lesser will have work, the books will dissappear, but the lesser also will read, they misluck in the thought to be wise, because they have not learned to criticize, and have not taught themselves to handle self critic, they are dreamy babies then, manipulated by a machine, maybe IF Trump will raise, this will be their first and last Big Baby fart in USA. They will then leave the rest world in chaos and war, and don't care, just make a business thing out of it, have you heard it ? that coward wants to raise all taxes to every single product entering USA from outside 200%, stupid cow i would call that idiot, he has too much honey milk in his brain, but none who milks his sick brain !

162

If you get no respect,
but epileptics in crash helmets
are allowed to act authoritatively towards you.
If you are unmarried and are the scapegoat,
not the competent employee,
and you are denied a wage yourself.
If they want to be chaste,
stay at home, but send their husband,
for a low-value feeling,
to ruin your reputation.
If their path always goes downhill,
drive you away, chase you to the churchyard,
serve you contempt in the morning,
their personal sorrow at lunchtime,
serve you a toast in the evening,
ALL THEIR YES-IN people.....
then you have enjoyed German culture!

When everyone is against you, turn around and you will become the leader.

With whom are priests...
in the best hands?

They like to be freed,
from their addiction to sex,
they feel under pressure, they always have it on,
how many times a day do they do it,
they get it on, perhaps with professional ladies,
in hiding in the house of worship,
to cast off their shame,
to talk openly about their obsessions,
with a woman who knows her body,
who knows it like Santa Claus,
after all, they all want to be freed !

Firstly, daughter doesn't take drugs.
Secondly, daughter doesn't know jealousy.
Thirdly, daughter doesn't bring
father a bastard into the marriage.
Fourthly, daughter doesn't stop at nothing.
Fifthly, daughter has no plans of her own,
the patriarch goes to a sex therapist, he cheats on her,
the daughter scares off every suitor,
then, as someone who came too late,
with his money, the new apartment, as a gift with concessions,
the desire for grandchildren, or even two !

Someone told me, "If you were obedient to the king, you wouldn't live in a
hut." I told him, "If you knew how to live in a but, you wouldn't have
obeyed the king."

What is fitting for a king? What are young people today?
I'll tell you... it is not important to them
that life is only earned through work,
that life is about human aspects,
that the old people showed them how it was
who learned that working their backs off is normal,
who know it openly even in old age, work
that can give in gratitude for life,
like children today can no longer say thank you,
like the joy of mothers for growing life,
how it is all the same to them to face life,
where young people look at their mothers from behind,
with the rear end first and step out,
with the awareness of guide dogs,
with ignorance strive after kings
who pretend to be blind to the grown
flowers that are their mothers,
recieve their love, and fuck them off.

What is attractive to you in a potential partner?
He might have known a lot about those women he had,
and cares with honesty about it.
He could give answers of experience,
about matters of me is interested,,
and shows an interest in get to know me.
He learned to care for the garden, house
all about children matters, and knows about the worth of life.
He taught himself to share about matters of friends,
and gives himself as human, and not as a king !
THAT IS ALL HUMAN, what i want.

EMBARRASSING.....
A father who gives up his house,
advertises his company called "broken",
his house, the child finds out,
lives in the shadows,
no one outside notices,
the little one at his side,
has his father-in-law...
look after his garden like a servant,
because anyone who is stupid enough to
give up an inheritance that is actually too early,
doesn't have to look after the flowers,
he should just do that himself!
So you see the little old woman standing there,
with her big bush,
and all that is visible to everyone outside is the roof,
that's how it should be..... huhhhh.

Where there is no king, there is no suffering,
where there is no half-measure, there is no ignorance,
where there is no arrogance, there is no self-righteousness,
where there is no remorse, there is no solidarity.

THE "WAY" of creating POVERTY!
Planning child expropriations in advance, before the child is born,
using violence, bringing together the traumatized,
subjecting them to stigma and persecution, stalking and bullying,
proselytizing, discriminating, then suppressing them
for a good twenty years and keeping them "unemployed" by force,
statistically suppressed, inciting hatred, a mother-child breach,
there is sometimes a huge gap
between "legal" and "humane", Mr. Nemitz!
We know the existing Nazi law in the country.

There will some more years pass, until that day would come,
to bring another democratic law to the publicity, tells
"the stealing babies from all even half born german kids are totally legal" ?
Today is not a single lawyer able to criticize or go against the fact, they say.

Like my brains say "I only repeat back that body is right handed; I'm not all
plants and animals in a paradox of everything = nothing" :) .... try this in
another language, reading left to right (handedness): the future in general,
including dreams and night and day dreams, is perfectly vague as it belongs
to all future pointers: 1+1 = 2 specific, coordinated points: #handedness =
#now = #forever= "physical ± bodies ± connected" , "the end" of what
movie is "the only end for every other one",
so the role of imagination is to imagine a healthier planet for all observers,
including younger plants and animals = evolution = ethical preferences #life
= #like (vs suicide and murder, for instance, as sacrificing children to the
sun or some wack shit adult cultural pathology), simply observe that being
physical intelligences is now "neither alive (created) nor dead (destroyed)".

#handedness means I can't speak for another one, I can only hope physics
and biology go viral: we will always have (at least) I+I biological parents,
each.

I hope human adults will stop thinking we're all other plants and animals combined into some paradoxically (false) virtue-signaling abuse children's 1+1 =2 physical brain sides: "zero origin dollars = carpe diem = zero end" You are true. Thank you. I do not often find solidarity, but i am always in life that one telling the truth, as much lesser is the consequence that peopl try to listen to me. That Way People have to become big Artist one day, because you cannot build a node in Brain and prove them not to think, this will be a next english book from me...

I know every single bone in me. I feel each one of those veins bring me oxygen. I am shaking my thought with empathy and soul and music in speech. I will never give up my physically connection and will ever love more the way than the end of the road. Not to paint, sad but true but bring out to the puclic all this, causes much confrontation and pains, to go through, but you recieve many more insights with it, i know what you mean, but all people have the own movies to dream, i see some people may be sooo far, but as well as they are the same brain triggering and have same humors, that they are so fucking close again, we all come solidary to the similar brains easy as well as we all had once or twice the same aim at the end of the road, but had still to walk and a walk so long, that we started to enjoy the long walk more than the end of the ways, sometimes the Buddha is found in yourself, like you do too.

Yes, sometimes a dream image in the morning first was superflous or funny to see, but at the following day this was the essence of the daily teaching, like you said it, then you have reached the point to be arrived at nature, today was a raven from the top of a house downtown he spoke and sang to us the publicum, this was overwhelming.

As a writer, experienced in working with the disabled, ... I believe I would have been a good mother to my son, who was born on 11 August 1997 in the maternity ward in Kiel, and was hushed up, that I was denounced as pregnant, that my child was forcibly taken away from me immediately after birth, that lawyers made me aware that an old Nazi law was in effect, that declared every child removal "legal" without justification, that a lawyer had no authority, that my son was still abused in front of my eyes, and even then passed on from foster home to foster home, that when I got my son back, he had already told me about his abusive experiences in the shower when he was 2 years old.

ABROAD the church does this brazenly,
it illegally expropriates newborns, sells them for forced adoption,
declares them dead to their mothers, collects its money in all possible "areas" for this.... TO EACH OWNER HIS OWN WAY!

And just like i remembered those aquaintances of real people from Italy, here or everywhere, they are steadily liars at me, that one who confronted me very sudden with his dick pics, the one who forbid me the mouth as german musician and hippy in Italy, the other one who told me not to contact him directly Mr. Wilde the other musician, and the last who tried to carry me to church in his massive brain watering .... so tell yer, that Italian language won't be my interest, reading with translation sometimes but nothing else, i am not the one Deer for the italian hunters ! It is impossible to missionate me !

At the time of "Franco" and "Hitler" in western Europe it was said
"A woman must be married. A woman must have children.
A woman must obey her husband. A woman must not vote."
Their western European dictatorship therefore resorted to stealing babies from women and selling them to the highest bidder without children.
This has continued to this day, all over Europe children are stolen, sold and abused, as a lasting legacy from the time of the dictatorship, because the laws allow it ! Not a single lawyer has any objections to this.

Would I sit with another woman
around a hole
in the freezing snow on the frozen river
while fishing in the cold,
to "hang" him in there for a bit?
Asking her the question
"Did one go in?
Then just get him out again?"

and looking at the fat roast,
she looks down and says,
"No, I'll let him squirm a bit longer..."
has it ever occurred to a woman to act so stupidly?

If I, as a philosopher,
learn how I, as a daughter, fuck my mother,
then I was told I needed a psychologist, if I, as a
philosopher, see how my surroundings fuck
children, then these neighbors are called
pedophiles, then I consider everything together,
like me, unemployment, maybe God too, and
my soul, and everything around it, in that I
only concern myself with myself, being banned
from working, and consequently only knowing
myself, but the whole world doesn't care about
sin, and God doesn't watch anyone masturbate,
and they still rub themselves against children
today. That's why most people think they're
God, and want to be left undisturbed in their
activities.
This year's child is added, "CHOSEN", which is
normal, and afterwards everyone is always
disappointed, because they are much more
DISAPPOINTED with themselves!

I imagine how I would see it as a man myself
if women came to me early, whom I didn't even want to know,
I would whiz away from them like an arrow,
preferably by bicycle to the edges of the world,
to find freedom in the wilderness, I would always be up and away
so quickly that these wooers of youth and marriage-mad Stone Ages
who would grow old early, and their dreams would end
with me under the waterfall,
in a sight that was supposed to be the same,
like a herd of men only with long hair, and I meanwhile
always stand on the edge of what they are doing,
as a climbing flower reaching for the sun,
I would become a vine, a slender one,
and the women would become fat men who get their men married,
that they would feed the women, reproduce, eat, drink, reproduce,
maybe get rich, not much different from the animal world,
except that animals don't humiliate, even if they eat each other!

171

This sign says that the woman does not need a man for her dreams and their fulfillment, even if she only wakes up in the morning from a deep sleep to face the day when she will be useful !

The Middle Ages, folks, are not so far away! When my dear neighbor confirms to me how her own mother, as a young woman, had to leave home and go out into the world, working to survive, her only option was to do housework and prepare food for the rich, the fine people, and the useful craftsman from Romania does the actual work like today, and she said that a coachman himself was asked by the owner to be called "Madam" by him in future, and he replied "No, Madam, God may be as kind as he can be, but nobody needs that!" Even those who still want to take the right to put themselves in God's place, to be called that, that is so unbelievably stupid and unreal !

The idea of marriage is a traditional understanding of roles that is outdated! In Germany, it is not recommended to plan a marriage without first getting legal advice for the future! Women mistakenly rely on men for financial matters. Women earn less. Marriage is not a division of property. The housewife only owns the vacuum cleaner afterwards, in her simplicity, in good times and bad, hahaha, but what she has not earned does not belong to her. Marriage in this country is a "community of gain". The person who earns keeps the property alone. The housewife asks for what she needs every week. This hierarchy means that the earner has the sole say. Whoever has the money can decide on purchases and expenditure, manage the inheritance, increase the property, accumulate and spend, even go bankrupt, and does not have to account for it. More than 7% of women between 30 and 37 do not even have their own bank account. Women who rely on their husbands are stupid, they ask for household money and have to be paid for their sex and services. The idea of marriage is a trivial one, but you can't buy anything with an idea! And getting rid of it and lying to someone also means being completely financially at the mercy of someone in marriage, too, is falling for a simple calculation !

Marriage today is like having a bird in your hand rather than a pigeon on the roof, everyone has experienced this before, having been left behind. The romance is no longer there, well, if in the past the woman's father was asked, it was for a good reason, the woman was sold off like a commodity. The most tasteless wedding ceremony points to the most tasteless marriage, later the dress no longer fits, but the wrinkles fit on the face, letting go shortly afterwards to save face, to let him/her go! Work for women today: housework in marriage, looking out of the clean window, falling in love, then having children, ending up as a retired couple, like Cinderella in the mouse tower, intelligence, beauty, refinement reduced to being a couch potato, outside, Mr. "Papa's" successor could slay dragons on the battlefield, her life never resembled an adventure, just a new "possession".

People often say, "if we don't have anything else to say to each other, we might as well get married !"

I prefer to look those who are selling me friendship in the eye. Helps against nasty surprises! No, my skills with strangers are exhausted. The sooner they tease me, make me look stupid, and contact me now and again, reject me and then approach me again, is not what I want, so I am increasingly distancing myself from the games that concern me. I said at the beginning that I have no intention of forming a real relationship with strangers online. And I no longer trust the whole thing. Who knows, maybe you will find someone else who you can pressure into marrying you. I am not available! I no longer have the will to take in tourists, actually no one at all.

So I'm not doing it ! I've explained to people that I've realized for about half a year now that I'm incapable of being in a relationship, and I realize that I don't want to and can't have a partner by my side because it just doesn't work for me.

WHAT IS IT A SURPRISE TO ONE...

THAT THERE ARE NO PROFESSIONAL OPPORTUNITIES FOR DEDICATED WORK WITH THE CHURCH, or PERMANENT EMPLOYMENT?

The Pope is just as unselfish as all those who work for him. The Church lets normal, well-working employees with a humanitarian standard spend years slaving away for contracts, blackmailing the chronically ill with false promises and church double standards for the doubly suffering workforce, ruining careers by requiring medication, but by ratting out others, postponing the risk of being fired, and by allowing workers to have a say, immediately terminating the contract for continued employment.

HEIKE THIEME - YLVA -

I am offering TRILOGY!

1 Emancipation

2 Knowledge of human nature

3 Detachment

Be successful -

Don't let anything happen to you,

whoever falls before you will be them !

My theory of "the big bang until now" is short, we just spoke about of our theory what was first, the egg or the chicken, then i told them shortsaid my version, and the both had many things to complain, was funny, at least we closed that all in the world wether they are muslim, christian or viking, nature believers or even living in an african cave, and on island they all do believe in the right way they want to, and all things to believe in a better future for their region they live in, and none is better than another not the region nor the people with their believe, one friend's wonderful saying and wording from the Koran made me happy very much. Those both kids, brothers are the kids of the single parent father. It feels good having that understanding between, not many think it over, so that everyone may speak and talk with everyone.

1. was the tree
2. was the worm eat the apple from the tree
3. was the worm lay eggs
4. was the worm becoming a snake
5. the snake grew to a raptile
6. the raptile got wings and flew
7. while the fish in the sea climbed on earth
8. the new land citizan got a fur and four legs
9. later on the mammal was also calles human

so my theory is first was the egg, then was the chicken !
"Would you like to sit at the right hand of the Lord in paradise, bathing in His grace and ecstatically enjoying eternal life?" "No."

Hypocrisy! They may hypocritically protect churches to save them from dccay, they may depopulate the countryside, the farmers may go bankrupt and move to the cities, they ensure a careful image of preserving the "old", but on the contrary, as with everything that ages, there is usually nothing left but sand and stones, because where would the church be if it were about displaced persons, asylum seekers and the poor rural population, about wanderers and lonely travelers, if no one was living there anymore anyway? but what room ? I find the most old buildings now are rotten, so how would the Pteridactyl want ever stay inside with us ?

Back in the light

Beautiful and constant, frosty and floating in space, humorous and inviting
to dream, sparkling element knowing about ideas, locked behind a door,
strong in experience, knowledge experienced, coupled and complementary
as a whole, free even, for whom your opinion is divided, your face presents
itself. You had to experience some things, and in the end give back.
Behind walls it seems purple. My views have gathered.

My portrait. I am building my universe, not denouncing the environment,
but still strong and my art can hold its own. Have the courage to use your
mind, to reach for the wooden post in a movement of the living and happily
reach a shore. To reach worlds to be explored, to the universes, to attain
fiction and to understand the use of reality. We want to travel in the sun
immediately and be involuntarily drawn into fascination by simply
observing.

Flax in flat lands

Cherry sweet cake, let's try it. The euphoria of two people, everyone left
behind, the guitar being played into the child's arms, the looks a little
threatening, their expressions difficult to understand. But he who hears their
song will do it.

The space must have additional dimensions, to see only a daring, bizarre
idea, of something that is a completely natural explanation, left, right, back,
front, top, bottom and time. To doubt that everything is very simple, if
perhaps the missing dimension is not seen. Waves and dents that spread in
space are imaginable, recognizable and visible up close. Energies that roll
up in our atomic vision, not easy to understand, but twisted, rolled, pulled
apart. Just as one knows how to walk around the world, one knows how to
explore the dimensions of this world. Form can mean many things and
change interior space and sounds, but aren't there also subliminal forces that
swing and vibrate in a curvature.

Numbers that give the universe its properties, stronger atomic movement can erase all of this. To put it precisely, the solution lies in sixth dimensions, that the theory offers itself as one for everything and for nothing, we find ourselves in the eleventh dimension.

Yerba Santa

Thoughts and feelings oscillate in our brain. We don't see the world as it really is, no, we construct a model that is most likely for us to understand the world. Our own theories help us to understand. We are constantly doing science. We work politically, religiously, commercially, create a world with power and passion, and use this power to answer questions about our worldview and everything that moves us.

Snake feathers

Who has not searched for the philosopher's stone on all the beaches of the world in an instant? He has looked for all the ways to discover it on the edge, the master who looks within himself. And when he lifts up the stones that they threw at me among the flowers, it is always easier to remember his quick words, to remember the colors of childhood and to put the past before the future. To achieve success rather than to think about what is to come and to feel what it is like right now. It is important to find answers to these questions, like holding your child in your arms. A glance around a lake and to start living for yourself, to arrange the number of feelings, knowing that this is how to build a bridge for yourself.

What remains

It is worrying about my society, which dares to lump together individuality, roots, resources and people who act or people who think, and wants to see everything in the same way. If not even I, the individual, am prepared to take the key to my dream from anyone. Who is not more capable of doing this than the individual himself?

177

Back to the origin

Two people who loved each other hid in a raft. They separated from their families and floated down a river, unprotected against the fall of its falls. It turned into a rock that was whipped by the water. They plunged into the depths, and neither of them ever returned. For one, loneliness is something undesirably unpleasant, and for the other, perhaps for this reason, irreplaceable. On the beach, I feel as small as a beetle. My steps go heavy across the land. On the coast near the city, the bright lights brush against me. When I wander past berry bushes on the North Sea, longing is intertwined with a reunion along the wind turbines.

Whose face I saw lies in the distance, rugged beaches prevented me from reaching out. Geese are easy to spot, but not the trust of a friend. There have been a few strange men in my life, sweet, good-looking and intelligent at the same time. It's not about the great love that could have given me the impetus in life, it seemed more like a detoxification cure to me to find my way in a strange world of men.

Look at yourself!

It, the love that unites the two halves of our nature. Zeus had asked for it from mankind, his weapons the thoughts that rage against them. To create mankind for himself and to cover them with an image that they did not wish for, and to shape for himself the gray thoughts of the distant past that erupt like wars. A bit of both, part woman, part man, the form of the synthesis of both, in contrast to the in-between world, in which the latter is always looking to unite and preserve its human characteristics. How is it not easier to make things easier for the masses if you take away their rights?

Gø hva du tøs !

Do what you want ! I too had a wide-ranging and fulfilling life. I learned to think, experience, see and speak in feminine terms, dreamed of a positive world. In many cases I took the initiative, and looking back, I was able to be tough and yet it still seemed touching to friends. I don't have to hide my feelings and my knowledge from the world. It's as if I can tolerate the people around me. That's who I am, empathetic, observant, distant, assessing. And it took a long time to form a part of this society around me in this life, even when it was raining outside and the cold crept under my clothes.

Shadow thieves

It is not a religion that imprisons a spirit because it does not want diversity. Everyone exists side by side from their own center. You grow in beauty. The light, the belief in yourself, the strength to recognize in your heart, to always start anew, to develop in a beautiful life, the chance to do so is available to everyone where there is progress. When strangers give each other a smile, people shake hands. So in this life I got to feel a part of a society, as a woman, as a troubadour, in my speeches, along with the people, dream images and the happiness of life. And I knew that if I borrow a piece of eternity, I must continue to work on it and try to make the best of it.

My soul becomes a tree

It is they who ride the highest waves and who are always welcome to everyone. Most of the time, all that was left behind was a pile of broken glass, a few graves and smashed tires. This only encourages you to start your engine somewhere else and never look back in life. Child, you are gifted with authenticity, you will find your way among wolves. You may show them the way one day, and you won't have to make an effort to follow in their footsteps, because you know how valuable and irreplaceable a life is!

My soul becomes a tree

They are the ones who ride the highest waves and are always welcomed by everyone. Most of the time, all that remains is a pile of broken glass, a few graves and smashed tires. Which only encourages you to start your engine somewhere else and never look back in life. Child, you are gifted with authenticity, you will find your way among wolves. You may show them the way one day, and you won't have to make an effort to follow in their footsteps because you know how valuable and irreplaceable life is!

The world is not just subjective. The world is changeable. Like the medium of art, it leads most people into a projection hole. You project yourself into it and experience the world as a model. And reality is only a construction and can only ever be interpreted. The basis of things is so crucially constant, whether something is real or not, it only ends in a suggested experience.

It depends on how the world becomes negotiable?
How does it become open and inclusive instead of closed and exclusive?
Love is sometimes too far away

First came trust, then intelligence. We humans remained childlike, with round, pink faces and small mouths. We swear like dogs bark. What wolves only do in their childhood. Our childlike curiosity made us tolerant and trusting towards the world. Far away from our wild relatives, we learned to trust each other. Our youthful temperament taught us to solve our problems. Becoming human only happens in human temperament. We only became smart when we became social. We should only preserve a friendly, open temperament like that of our children. Where fixed rules and cooperation required people to grasp the world with curiosity and tolerance, this made us dependent on bonds.

A universe fit in a bag

The engine was still running and if you wanted to be a rock star, you would have already cried because nobody liked you there either. I'm sorry, it seems to me that I don't see it that way. And if they are no longer inside you, then there is already one less in the midst of love. Those who dare to tell me that a couple in love refreshes themselves every year, then at most in the bath water of other clean people, then I no longer need love, of course! Travel and comfort until a meal is expensive again. A long way ahead of you, an actor in search of a goal. Your fib is sympathetic, you are related to the sun, you shine right through it. You spread your laughter into the world, you know what lies behind it, and you won't have to change for anyone.

Fantasy's rivers Aspeola Odurata -

your amazement, an unbelievable feeling. To sail through the world and survive, to find your architecture and to beautify a world - and if they pick everything apart, I rise in all directions, they will no longer turn into birds because their innocence is lost. To dream requires years of work, to which they never submit.

At the end of a path

Some crowds are no different, some move in paths around the island of people, and those who like to talk to them are at home in many places, gestures and situations, because a place that you have left behind no longer holds you in anything. They are all looking for the great love, and they cannot find the trace. If the first one doesn't have it, the second one lacks it, in the end everyone lacks it, and aren't they vainly in a bad mood when everything doesn't work out on its own? Prince's son, look, Juan! What is he doing? And then what? Love for a label. What only a few can express linguistically. What is between us. What is more than a word ?
What remains of such an encounter? I associate nothing with that !

See Feathered Leaf

To have the power of a king is to look like a king. A just power goes with the truth, the only true authority comes from respect. Those who cowardly make pacts, who represent an ethics of conviction, with a character that is often imitated, with a conditioning that is unparalleled and with a penchant for utopia, no longer have the majority because everyone now understands the difference between mince and cake, between sugarcoating and cursing. Indians. Dispossessed of their own thinking. In a culture within the overproduction crisis of capitalism. At a standstill, infusion that follows standstill. Until I became part of the mess. Mass unemployment on a global scale. The fictitious capital was inflated in an illusion in which everything was destroyed again. In fear of the end of democracy? A financial simulation in which capital can accumulate on its own. Does anyone want to be fair? Hard to see. There are no more conflicts, they never talk to each other. In a depressing demonstration, they point out a lack of politics that completely lacks competence and understanding.

I guess I knew

I didn't know the reason at the beginning of the words, not right from the first hour. As I moved between the worlds, I recognized many people who prevented themselves from dreaming. So I definitely didn't need anyone else to convince me in a civilized and Christian way, to condition me, to put me in my place or to change me into an altruist. Life is where the unreal becomes reality and in reality it is possible to experience something of the dream, to discover the deep meaning of life on a path of life where only the path is the destination. Who prevents themselves from dreaming? They have always remained in the shadows. Their only desire is for wealth, which they do not have. Even less that they are entitled to it. Someone would offer you a poisoned biscuit to offer the city their only smile.

I guess I would know

I didn't know the reason at the beginning of the words, not right from the first hour. As I moved between the worlds, I recognized many people who prevented themselves from dreaming. Therefore, I definitely didn't need anyone else to convince me in a civilized and Christian way, to condition me to shit, to put me in my place or to change me into an altruist. Life takes place where the unreal becomes reality and in reality it is possible to experience something of the dream, to discover the deep meaning of life on a path of life where only the path is the destination. Who prevents themselves from dreaming? They have always remained in the shadows throughout their days. Their only desire is for prosperity, which they do not possess. Even less that they are entitled to it. Someone would offer you a poisoned biscuit in order to offer the city their only smile.

Change of tide - sublime in magic

A mother's confession, my first joke that I was able to remember about it, my last when the last bite goes down my throat. Children conceived in love and grown up with love. So those who love each other shake hands, and what is created in love will be connected. A path is clear, not too far from the steps, I tried not to avoid German social conditions and the act of single parenting.

There are successful catcher in the rye, the woman recognizes the vagabond. With all due respect, this is something that is burning on everyone's minds, to grow up once and for all and find friends! I didn't want to be a woman for you, I didn't want any of that. But I would have had enough of you. I didn't want to be your wife, not just any woman. My goal was just to be yourself. I didn't want to trade my skills for a relationship. It's not about loving someone for their mistakes. So one day I will teach others with my art to experience more of reality. In simplicity, it doesn't experience peace for so long, as if it would only fail to change a world for itself.

Excitingly Agitated

Anyone who knows the situations in their life also knows how long it will take, how the fire burns inside of you, until spaces have been created that you walk through a thousand times. If only those from outside would keep coming, who are dying to take away your sense of self. I have always wanted to get to know friends by giving them the space to create something for themselves.

Treasure hunt

The landscape in front of you opens up again, and all the details become visible. I feel the wind blowing through me like waves, and the salt of the sea greets me. So nature has me again. And only in this way did my thoughts learn to take a leap. The prospects for this are rosy, because I am learning to increase my strength again and to rely on myself. I too stand there alone among many and know that there is a secret behind everything. And knowing this leads to harmony.

Only the best for you

Who does their duty? Whether an avalanche breaks loose ultimately depends on whether a single snowflake falls, a tiny little snowflake, or a tiny little 'yes' instead of a 'no', or a signature that should not have been signed. Perhaps it also sounds like an echo in a fog where there are no more spectators, no noise, no applause. And sometimes you risk more if you don't take any risks, just to give yourself courage. They swear by their theories, but they don't care about the rest of the world. They want to persecute people with the help of symbolism, exterminate them, so to speak, and only get excited when they flee into their mother's arms, back into their womb, and dream of the wine, of which they need much more than they needed to bear the fact that they could have afforded so much wine had they never made their mistakes.

Man, Clara!

Precisely so that you don't get stuck in despair at one point in art. I know a lot about life and about education. I know how to assess my problems and how to end them, where and how they arise, and I think I offered my son a far more loving home than the one I experienced. And the fact that I wanted to move my home towards emotional openness in the most sensitive way possible only meant that I had not failed in life and, unlike my father, had been far more successful as a human being than he was. Only the imagination knows how to separate good from bad. You shouldn't lose yourself in your dreams. Your strength lies in not believing that your dreams will come true forever. And you set yourself the goal of gathering experiences that are tied to old things, that way you survive a part of your childhood and you keep a door open to keep your resistance to evil alive.

Love Exit - Flying Love!

I have my lust, the gift comes from my body.
I set my own goals.
I know how to change, it's not about me,
to let myself be socially absorbed
and undergo a partnership by mutual agreement,
just because they asked me to,
so I can sleep better, not to live in fear and insecurity,
to stand in love as abandoned.
In reality, people have not sunk as deep as we fear.
They just never got as high as we thought they were.
A beauty wilts like a flower,
is beauty power? Power wilted like a flower.

A democracy wilted if not cared for.
World of the vernissage, therapeutic elite
of spoiled children and grandchildren, grandchildren's grandchildren,
the car keys belong to the daughter,
the power of money thinks everything and everyone is dear,
who buys love for cash, the born sugar daddy,
the selfies hang monumentally through the house,
the other people are little caricatures.
Raped women... she can be so badly damaged,
and abandoned by her family, with nothing left to stand on,
but she can think, but she will flee,
even if she had family and the support of someone,
but then she would start to think, but then she would flee,
these mega pigs and this family would stalk her,
incapacitate her, persecute her, control her, denounce her,
but then she would think,
but she would never come back!

« HEIKE THIEME »

Das LEBEN ist ein LIED - aber die LIEBE ist die MUSIK !
Leider gehört dazu,
dass es in der MUSIK auch UNTERTÖNE GIBT !

LIFE is a SONG - but LOVE is MUSIC !
Unfortunately,
there are also UNDERTONES in MUSIC !

« HEIKE THIEME – YLVA »

Ich nutze in der Not gute Meditation, dann auch meine Frauensachen wie Soja, Aloe,
Ursalz, viel Wasser trinken, Energie aus Afa-Algen, immer in Bewegung bleiben, frische
Luft, keine Süßigkeiten, kein Alkohol, keine Drogen, ein paar gute Kräuter
für die Blase, Leinsamen für den Darm, Kohletabletten gegen Vergiftungen und
eigentlich entgiften Sie mit allem und zwar jeden Tag !
Ich sage -
Hab ein schönes Leben und genieße diesen Tag !
Aber im Moment befinde ich mich in einer Ruhephase für alles, was kommen würde,
und lasse den Rest, der war, hinter mir und schreibe an einem anderen Buch.
Selbstfürsorge bedeutete besser gesagt, ich war nie süchtig, Trauma ist eine Sache
meines ganzen Lebens, ich war nie deprimiert, Angst war nie mein Problem, akute
Schmerzen löse ich mit Chakra-Meditation, Gymnastik und Bewegung, Spiritualität ist
mein ganzes Leben und Bewusstsein ist des Seins bewusst zu leben,
dass ich nie etwas verpasst habe.

Also guten Tag !

I use good meditation in need, then also my woman things like Soy, aloe, original salt,
drinking lots of water, energy from Afa algae, always keep moving, fresh air, no
sweets, no alcohol, no drugs, a few good herbs for the bladder, linseed for the
intestines, charcoal tablets against poisoning , and you actually detoxify with
everything and every day !
I say -
Have a nice life, and enjoy that day !
But at moment I am in a resting phase, for all that would come, and leave the rest
that was, and write on another book. Selfcare better said meant, addicted I never was,
trauma is a whole life thing, depressed I never was, anxiety was never my problem,
acute pains I solve with chakra meditation, gymnastic, and moving, spirituality is
my whole life and consciousness is being aware, that I never missed.

Sothen Good Day !

EPILOGUE

HEIKE THIEME - YLVA -

Ich biete an TRILOGIE !
1 Emanzipation
2 Menschenkenntnis
3 Abnabelung

Seid erfolgreich -
Lasst Euch nichts gefallen,
wer vor Euch fällt, werden sie sein !

Wieder im Licht

Schön und konstant, frostig und schwebend im Raum, in Humor und
einladend zum Träumen, prickelndes Element wissend um der Ideen,
verschlossen hinter einer Tür, stark in Erfahrung, Wissen erlebt, im Ganzen
gekoppelt und komplementär, selbst frei, für den sich deine Meinung teilt,
bietet sich dein Angesicht. Manches musstest du erleben, und am Ende gib
zurück.

Hinter Mauern scheint es violett

Meine Ansichten haben sich gesammelt.
Mein Portrait. Ich baue an meinem Universum, nicht die Umgebung
anzuprangern, dennoch stark und meine Kunst kann sich halten. Habe Mut,
dich deines Verstandes zu bedienen, in einer Bewegung des Lebendigen
nach dem Holzpfahl zu greifen und glücklich an ein Ufer zu gelangen. In zu
erforschende Welten bis zu den Universen hinaus zu gelangen, Fiktion zu
erlangen und den Gebrauch der Wirklichkeit zu verstehen. Unmittelbar
wollen wir in der Sonne reisen und im bloßen Beobachten unwillkürlich zur
Faszination hingerissen werden.

Flachs in flachen Landen

Kirschsüßer Kuchen, lass es versuchen. Das Hochgefühl zu zweit, alle abgehängt, dem Kind wird die Gitarre in die Arme gespielt, die Blicke ein bisschen bedrohlich, ihre Miene schwer verständlich. Er wird es aber schon machen, der ihren Gesang erhört.

Der Raum muss zusätzliche Dimensionen haben, zu sehen nur eine gewagte, bizare Idee, von etwas, was eine ganz natürliche Erklärung, links, rechts, hinten, vorn, oben, unten und die Zeit. Daran zu zweifeln, es verhielt sich alles ganz einfach, wenn vielleicht die fehlende Dimension nicht gesehen wird. Wellen und Dellen, welche sich im Raum ausbreiten, sind vorstellbar, erkennbar und sichtbar ganz aus der Nähe. Energien, die sich aufrollen in unserer Atomsicht, nicht leicht zu verstehen, aber verdreht, gerollt, auseinandergezogen. Wie einer um die Welt weiß zu spazieren, weiß einer die Dimension dieser Welt zu erforschen. Form kann vieles bedeuten und Innenraum und Töne verändern, schweben da aber nicht auch unterschwellig Kräfte, die in einer Verkrümmung schwingen und vibrieren. Zahlen, die dem Universum seine Eigenschaften verleihen, stärker atomare Bewegung kann dies alles löschen. Präzise formuliert in sechsten Dimensionen liegt die Lösung, dass sich die Theorie bietet als eine für alles und für gar nichts, finden wir uns wieder in der elften Dimension.

Yerba Santa

Gedanken und Gefühle oszillieren in unserem Gehirn. Wir sehen die Welt nicht wie sie wirklich ist, nein, wir konstruieren ein Modell, das für uns am wahrscheinlichsten ist, die Welt zu verstehen. Unsere eigenen Theorien helfen uns zu verstehen. Wir sind ständig wissenschaftlich tätig. Wir erarbeiten uns politisch, religiös, kommerziell, erschaffen eine Welt mit Macht und Leidenschaft, beantworten uns in dieser Kraft die Fragen über unsere Weltsicht und all das, was uns bewegt.

Schlangengefieder

Wer suchte nicht in einem Augenblick den Stein der Weisen an allen Stränden dieser Welt ? Der schaute alle Wege, ihn am Rand zu entdecken, den Meister, der in einem selber schaut. Und hebt er unter Blumen die Steine empor, mit denen sie nach mir warfen, ist es immer leichter, sich an seine schnellen Worte zu erinnern, sich an die Farben der Kindheit zu erinnern und Vergangenheit vor Zukunft zu schieben. Erfolge zu erringen, als an Kommendes zu denken und zu spüren, wie es ist gerade jetzt. Gelten Antworten darauf zu finden, wie sein Kind im Arm zu halten. Ein Blick umrundet einen See und für sich Leben zu beginnen, die Zahl an Gefühlen zurecht zu legen, darum wissend sich eine Brücke zu erschaffen.

Was bleibt

Es macht besorgt bezüglich meiner Gesellschaft, welche Individualität, Wurzeln, Ressourcen und Menschen, welche handeln oder Menschen, die denken - wagt in einen Topf zu werfen und alles in allem gleich betrachten will. Wenn nicht mal ich der Einzelne von niemandem bereit bin, den Schlüssel zu meinem Traum zu übernehmen. Wer ist dazu nicht mehr in der Lage, als der Einzelne selbst ?

Zum Ursprung zurück

Zwei, die sich liebten, verbargen sich im Floß. Sie sich von ihrer Familie trennten, flossen auf einem Fluss dahin, gegen den Sturz seiner Fälle ungeschützt. Verwandelte er sich in einen Felsen, der von den Wassern gepeitscht wurde. Sie stürzten in die Tiefe, die beiden kamen nie wieder zurück. Für den Einen die Einsamkeit etwas unerwünscht Unangenehmes, und für den Anderen vielleicht aus diesem Grund Unersetzliches. Am Strand fühl' ich mich klein wie die Käfer. Über' s Land gehen meine Schritte schweren Gangs. An der Küste stadtnah streifen mich die leuchtenden Lichter. Streife ich vorbei an Beerensträuchern an der Nordsee, verflicht sich die Sehnsucht mit einem Wiedersehen entlang der Windanlagen.

Liegt in der Ferne wessen Gesicht ich sah, zerklüftete Strände hinderten mich zuzugreifen. Gänse leicht zu entdecken, aber das Vertrauen eines Freundes nicht. Es gab ein paar merkwürdige Männer in meinem Leben, zugleich süße, gut aussehende und intelligente. Es geht ja nicht um die große Liebe, die mir im Leben hätte den Antrieb geben können, es war mir eher wie eine Entschlackungskur vorgekommen in einer fremden Welt der Männer zurecht zu kommen.

Schau auf Dich !

Sie, die Liebe, welche die zwei Hälften unserer Natur vereint. Messerscharf hatte Zeus es sich vom Menschen erbeten, seine Waffen die Gedanken, die ihnen grollten. Sich den Menschen zu schaffen und mit einem Überbild zu überdecken, welches sie sich nicht herbei gewünscht, und für sich allein zurecht zu formen die grauen Gedanken in grauer Vorzeit, die sich wie Kriege überschlagen. Etwas von beiden, ein Teil von Frau, ein Teil von Mann, die Form der Synthese beider, entgegen der Zwischenwelt, in der welche immer danach auf der Suche, sich zu vereinen, und seine Eigenschaften als Mensch in sich zu bewahren. Wie geht es nicht leichter nach der Masche, es mit der Masse sich zu vereinfachen, wenn man ihnen die Rechte nähme ?

Gø hva du tøs !

Tu, was du willst ! Auch ich hatte ein weitgespanntes und erfülltes Leben. Ich lernte im Weiblichen zu denken, zu erfahren, zu sehen, zu sprechen, erträumte mir eine positive Welt. In vielen Fällen ward ich initiativ, und sehe ich zurück, konnte ich mich beinhart geben, und wirkte es auf Freunde dennoch rührend. Meine Gefühle und mein Wissen muss ich vor einer Welt nicht verstecken. Es ist, als könnte ich die Menschen um mich herum ertragen. So ist das, wie ich bin, einfühlend, beobachtend, distanziert, einschätzend. Und es dauerte lang, in diesem Leben einen Teil dieser Gesellschaft um mich zu bilden, auch wenn es draußen regnete und die Kälte mir unter die Kleidung kroch.

Schattendiebe

Es ist nicht eine Religion, die einen Geist einsperrt, da sie die Vielfalt nicht will. Alle bestehen nebeneinander aus der eigenen Mitte. Wächst man in Schönheit. Das Licht, den Glauben zu sich selbst, die Kraft im Herzen zu erkennen, stets neu zu beginnen, sich in einem schönen Leben zu entfalten, die Chance dazu gilt jedem, wo es Fortschritt gibt. Schenken Fremde sich ein Lächeln reichen Menschen sich die Hand. So bekam ich in diesem Leben einen Anteil einer Gesellschaft zu spüren, als Frau, als Troubadour, in meinen Reden, mitsamt den Menschen, Traumgebilden und dem Lebensglück. Und ich wusste, leihe ich mir ein Stück von der Ewigkeit, so muss ich auch weiter daran arbeiten und versuche, das Beste daraus zu schaffen.

Meine Seele wird ein Baum

Es sind sie, die auf den höchsten Wellen reiten und die stets an allen die Willkommenen sind. Zurück blieben meist nur Scherbenhaufen, ein paar Gräber und zusammen gefahrene Reifen. Was nur dazu ermuntert, seinen Motor woanders in Gang zu setzen und im Leben niemals auch nur zurück zu sehen. Kind, du bist mit Echtheit begabt, du wirst deinen Weg unter Wölfen finden. Du wirst ihnen vielleicht den Weg eines Tages weisen, und du brauchtest dich nicht anzustrengen in ihre Fußstapfen zu treten, weil du darum weißt, wie wertvoll und unaustauschbar ein Leben ist !

Die Welt ist nicht nur subjektiv. Die Welt ist veränderbar. Wie mit dem Mittel zur Kunst führt es die meisten in ein Projektionsloch. Man projiziert sich selbst hinein und erfährt die Welt als ein Modell. Und Realität ist nur eine Konstruktion und immer nur interpretierbar. Die Basis der Dinge ist so entscheidend stetig, ob etwas real ist oder nicht, endet es nur in einer suggerierten Erfahrung.

Es kommt darauf an, wie wird die Welt verhandelbar ?
Wie wird sie offen und einschließend, statt geschlossen und ausschließend ?

Liebe ist manchmal viel zu weit weg

Erst kam das Vertrauen, dann die Intelligenz. Wir Menschen blieben kindlich, runde, rosa Gesichter, kleiner Mund. Wir schimpfen, wie Hunde bellen. Was Wölfe nur in ihrer Kindheit tun. Unsere kindliche Neugier ließ uns duldsam und vertrauensvoll der Umwelt begegnen. Entfernt von unserer wilden Verwandtschaft lernten wir einander zu vertrauen. Unser jugendliches Temperament erst lehrte uns unsere Probleme zu lösen. Menschwerden erfolgt nur in menschlichem Temperament. Klug wurden wir erst, als wir sozial wurden. Erst ein freundliches, offenes Temperament, wie das unserer Kinder sollten wir bewahren. Was feste Regeln und Zusammenarbeit verlangte, so erfassten die Menschen die Welt mit Neugier und Verträglichkeit, dies ließ uns auf Bindung angewiesen sein.

Ein Universum passte in einen Beutel

Der Motor immer noch in Gang und wolltest du ein Rockstar werden, heultest du zuvor schon ab, weil auch da dich keiner mag. Tut mir Leid, ist es mir, als sehe ich das so nicht. Und wenn es sie in dir drinnen nicht mehr gibt, ist ja schon einer weniger inmitten der Liebe drin. Die mir zu sagen wagen, ein Liebespaar erfrischt sich jedes Jahr, dann höchstens im Badewasser anderer sauberer Leute, dann benötige ich die Liebe nicht mehr, klar ! Reisen und Trost bis eine Mahlzeit wieder teuer. Vor dir ein langer Weg, Schauspieler auf der Suche nach einem Ziel. Dein Flunkern sympathisch, bist mit der Sonne verwandt, strahlst mitten durch sie hindurch. Streust dein Lachen in die Welt, weißt um das Dahinter, und wirst dich für niemanden ändern müssen.

Fantasien' s Flüsse Aspeola Odurata -
dein Erstaunen, ein unglaubliches Gefühl. Durch die Welt zu segeln und zu bestehen, deine Architektur zu finden und eine Welt zu verschönern - und zerpflücken sie alles, erhebe ich mich in alle Richtungen, sie werden sich nicht mehr in Vögel verwandeln, weil ihre Unschuld ist verspielt.
Zu träumen braucht es Jahre Arbeit, derer sie sich unterwerfen nie.

Am Ende eines Wegs

Manche Masse ist nicht anders, manche sich in Wegen um die Insel der Menschen bewegen, und der, der sich gern mit ihnen unterhält, ist zu hause an vielen Orten, Gesten und Situationen, weil dich ein Ort, den du zurück gelassen, in nichts mehr hält. Sind sie alle nach der großen Liebe auf der Suche, und sie finden darin nicht die Spur. Hat der Erste nicht, fehlt es dem Zweiten, am Ende fehlt es jedem, und sind sie nicht eitel schlecht gelaunt, wenn sich nicht alles von allein ergibt ? Prinzen Sohn, sieh da, der Juan ! Was tut er ? Und was dann ? Liebe für ein Etikett. Was sprachlich für nur wenige umzusetzen geht. Was sich zwischen uns befindet. Was steht mehr als ein Wort ? Was bleibt an einer solchen Begegnung ? Damit verbindet sich mir ein Nichts !

See Gefiedertes Blatt

Die Macht eines Königs zu besitzen, heißt wie ein König auszusehen. Eine gerechte Macht geht mit der Wahrheit die einzig wahre Autorität entsteht durch Respekt. Wer feige paktiert, Gesinnungsethik vertritt, in einer Prägung, welche gerne Nachahmer findet, einer Konditionierung, die Ihresgleichen sucht und einem Hang zur Utopie, speist heute keine Mehrheit mehr ab, weil ein jeder inzwischen zwischen Hack und Kuchen, zwischen Schönreden und Fluchen den Unterschied versteht.
Indianer. Vom eigenen Denken enteignet. In einer Kultur, innerhalb der Überproduktionskrise des Kapitalismus. Im Stillstand, Infusion, die auf den Stillstand folgt. Bis ich ein Teil des Kuddelmuddel geworden bin. Massenarbeitslosigkeit in Weltmaßstab. Das fiktive Kapital wurde aufgeblasen in einer Illusion, in der wieder alles zerstört ward. In Angst vor' m Ende der Demokratie ? Eine Finanzsimulation, in der das Kapital vor sich allein akkumulieren kann. Will da einer gerecht sein ? Schwer zu sehen. Es gibt keine Konflikte mehr, nie reden sie miteinander. In einer deprimierenden Demonstration, sie auf mangelnde Politik hinweisen, der die Kompetenz und ihr Verständnis gänzlich fehlt.

Ich schätze, Ich wüsste

Ich kannte nicht zu Anfangs der Worte Grund, nicht gleich zu erster Stunde.
Wo ich mich zwischen den Welten bewegte, erkannte ich viele Menschen,
die sich selbst am Träumen behinderten. Daher benötigte ich garantiert
keinen anderen, der mich zivilisiert, und christlich überzeugen müsste,
konditioniert zusammen scheißt, in Schranken verweist oder mich zum
Altruisten umändern müsste. Leben verläuft da, wo Unwirkliches in
Wirklichkeit und in der Wirklichkeit etwas vom Traum zu erleben geht, den
tiefen Sinn des Lebens zu entdecken auf einem Lebensweg, wo nur der Weg
das Ziel. Wer hindert sich selbst am Träumen ? Er ist seiner Tage nach stets
im Schatten geblieben. Sein einziges Wollen hängt am Wohlstand, den er
nicht besitzt. Noch weniger, dass es ihm zusteht. Einer würde dir einen
vergifteten Keks anbieten, um somit der Stadt sein einziges Lächeln zu
bieten.

Gezeitenwandel - im Zauber erhaben

Die Beichte einer Mutter, mein erster Witz, den ich darüber behalten konnte,
mein letzter, wenn der letzte Happen mir runter geht. Kinder, die in Liebe
gezeugt und mit Liebe erwachsen. So geben die sich einander die Hände,
die sich lieben, und verbunden wird sein, was in Liebe geschaffen. Ein Weg
frei, den Schritten nicht zu fern, versuchte ich keinen Bogen zu machen um
deutsche, soziale Verhältnisse und den Akt der Alleinerziehung.
Da gibt es erfolgreiche Fänger im Roggen, die Frau erkennt den
Vagabunden. Bei allem Respekt, dies brennt doch jedem auf den Nägeln,
einmalig erwachsen zu werden und Freunde zu finden ! Frau sein wollte ich
für dich nicht, nichts davon habe ich gewollt. Ich hätte aber auch genug von
Euch. Ich wollte nicht Eure Frau sein, nicht irgendeines welchen Frau. Nur
sich selbst sein war mein Ziel. Ich wollte nicht mein Können gegen eine
Beziehung tauschen. Es kommt nicht darauf an, jemanden für seine Fehler
zu lieben. So lehre ich die anderen mit meiner Kunst eines Tages, mehr von
der Wirklichkeit zu erfahren. Sie erlebt in Einfachheit so lange keine Ruhe,
als müsse sie daran nur scheitern, eine Welt für sich zu ändern.

Bannig Aufgewühlt

Wer die Situationen in seinem Leben kennt, weiß auch wie lange es dauern wird, wie das Feuer in einem brennt, bis sich Räume erschaffen haben, durch die man tausend Male geht. Würden nicht nur von außen immer wieder die ankommen, denen es auf der Leber brennt, dir dein Selbstverständnis zu nehmen. Wollte ich schon immer Freunde kennen lernen, indem ich ihnen den Raum überlasse, etwas für sich zu erschaffen.

Schatzsuche

Die Landschaft vor einem tut sich wieder auf, und alle Einzelheiten werden erkennbar. Ich fühle wellenartig den Wind durch mich wehen, und das Salz der See schenkt mir seinen Gruß. So hat mich die Natur wieder. Und nur so lernten meine Gedanken einen Sprung zu tun. Die Aussichten dafür sind rosig, denn ich lerne wieder meine Kräfte zu mehren und mich auf mich selbst zu verlassen. Auch ich stehe allein unter vielen einfach da und weiß, hinter allem verbirgt sich ein Geheimnis. Und darum zu wissen, führt zur Harmonie.

Für Dich nur das Beste

Wer tut seine Pflicht ? Ob eine Lawine losbricht, hängt zuletzt davon ab, ob eine einzige Schneeflocke mehr fällt, eine winzige, kleine Schneeflocke, oder ein winziges kleines 'Ja', statt einem 'Nein', oder eine Unterschrift, die nicht hätte geleistet werden dürfen. Vielleicht lautet es auch wie ein Hall in einem Nebel, in dem keine Zuschauer mehr, kein Lärm, kein Applaus. Und manchmal riskiert man mehr, wenn man kein Risiko eingeht, allein, um sich wieder Mut zu zusprechen. Sie schwören auf ihre Theorien, sie pfeifen jedoch auf den Rest der Welt. Mit Hilfe von Symbolik wollen sie Menschen verfolgen, quasi ausrotten, und erregen sich nur noch, wenn sie in Mutter' s Arme fliehen, zurück in den Leib und träumen von dem Wein, von dem sie noch viel mehr brauchen, als sie nötig hatten, um zu ertragen, dass sie sich soviel Wein hätten leisten können, hätten sie nie ihre Fehler begangen.

Mensch, Clara !

Gerade um in der Kunst nicht an einem Punkt verzweifelt stehen zu bleiben. Ich habe eine Menge Ahnung vom Leben und von der Erziehung. Ich weiß meine Probleme einzuschätzen und zu beenden, wo und wie sie auftauchen, und ich denke, ich habe meinem Sohn ein weitaus liebevolleres Zuhause geboten, als das, welches ich erlebte. Und damit, dass ich mein Zuhause auf die sensibelste Art und Weise zu einer emotionalen Offenheit bewegen wollte, hieß ja nur, dass ich am Leben nicht gescheitert bin und ihm Gegensatz zu meinem Vater, menschlich weit erfolgreicher gewesen bin als er. Nur die Fantasie weiß Gutes von Schlechtem zu trennen. Man soll sich in seinen Träumen nicht verlieren. Seine Stärke besitzt man darin, nicht zu glauben, dass die Träume bis in alle Ewigkeit wahr werden. Und man setzt sich zum Ziel, Erfahrungen zu sammeln, die an alte Dinge gebunden sind, so überlebt man ein Stück Kindheit, und man hält sich eine Tür offen, den Widerstand gegen Böses lebendig zu halten.

Liebesflucht - Love Exit Flying Love !

I have my lust, the gift comes from my body.
I set my own goals.
I know how to change, it's not about me,
to let myself be socially absorbed
and undergo a partnership by mutual agreement,
just because they asked me to,
so I can sleep better, not to live in fear and insecurity,
to stand in love as abandoned.
In reality, people have not sunk as deep as we fear.
They just never got as high as we thought they were.

Eine Schönheit wird welk wie eine Blume,
ist Schönheit denn Macht ? Welkte die Macht wie eine Blume.
Welkte eine Demokratie, die man nicht hegt und pflegt.
Welt der Vernissage, therapeutische Elite
der verwöhnten Kinder und Enkel, Enkelsenkel,
der Auto Schlüsse gehört der Tochter,
die Macht des Geldes hält alles und jeden für lieb,
der sich die Liebe gegen Bares kauft, der geborene Sugar-Daddy,
die Selfies hängen monumental durchs Haus,
die anderen Menschen sind kleine Karikaturen.
Vergewaltigte Frauen.. sie kann noch so zugerichtet sein,
und von Familie fallen gelassen,ohne alles stehen,
doch sie kann denken, doch sie wird fliehen,
selbst wenn sie Familie gehabt hätte und den Rückhalt von irgend einem,
doch dann begänne sie zu denken, doch dann würde sie fliehen,
diesen Mega Schweinen und würde diese Familie ihr nachstellen,
sie zu entmündigen, verfolgen, kontrollieren, denunzieren,
doch dann würde sie denken,
doch würde sie nie mehr zurück kommen !

« *HEIKE THIEME* »

198

Was mich kleiden würde.
Ich leiste Arbeit mit Verstand.
Ich bin gleichwertig wie ein Mann.
Ich bin nicht gefällig, aber mächtig.
Ich schließe mich keinen Rassisten an.
Ich verweigere den sexistischen Mann.
Rassisten und Sexisten sind Tyrannen.
Gäbe es kein Normdenken, kleidete ich mich anders.
Gäbe es kein Männerbewusstsein, arbeitete ich anders.
Gäbe es kein Patriarchat, dachte ich anders wie sie.
Ich entscheide wie ich Sex habe und mit wem.
Ich diskriminiere niemanden, also niemand mich.
Ich arbeite nur noch für gleichen Lohn.
Ich biete ihnen nur noch Kinder, für Gleichberechtigung.
Ich und nur ich kontrolliere meinen Körper.
Ich verhüte solange ich es will.
Ich darf ein Kind zu zeugen ablehnen.
Ich war für sie alle Jahre "Frau Schade !"
Aber seit heute werde ich ihnen nicht mehr dienen !

« HEIKE THIEME - YLVA »

What would dress me.
I do work with intelligence.
I am equal to a man.
I am not pleasing, but powerful.
I don't associate myself with any racists.
I refuse the sexist man.
Racists and sexists are tyrants.
If there were no norm thinking, I would dress differently.
If there were no male consciousness, I would work differently.
If there were no patriarchy, I would think differently than them.
I decide how I have sex and with whom.
I don't discriminate against anyone,
so no one discriminates against me.
I only work for equal pay.
I only offer them children, for equality.
I and only I control my body.
I'll use contraception as long as I want it.
I can refuse to father a child.
For all of them I was "Mrs. Shame !"
But as of today I will no longer serve them !